SERIOUS ABOUT LVE

OTHER BOOKS
BY
DR. KAY KUZMA

Belonging (Ken and Nancy Rockey with Kay Kuzma)

Between Hell and High Water (Kay Kuzma and Brenda Walsh)

Easy Obedience

The First 7 Years: Parenting With Strong Values and a Gentle Touch

Fit Forever

Mending Broken People

Passionate Prayer (Brenda Walsh with Kay Kuzma)

Passionate Prayer Promises (Brenda Walsh and Kay Kuzma)

Prayer Promises for Kids (Kay Kuzma and Brenda Walsh)

SERIOUS ABOUT
L♥VE

3ABN BOOKS

Three Angels Broadcasting Network
West Frankfort, Illinois
www.3abn.org

Pacific Press® Publishing Association
Nampa, Idaho
Oshawa, Ontario, Canada
www.pacificpress.com

You can obtain additional copies of this book by calling toll-free 1-800-765-6955 or by visiting http://www.adventistbookcenter.com.

3ABN BOOKS is dedicated to bringing you the best in published materials consistent with the mission of Three Angels Broadcasting Network. Our goal is to uplift Jesus Christ through books, audio, and video materials by our family of 3ABN presenters. Our in-depth Bible study guides, devotionals, biographies and lifestyle materials promote whole person health and the mending of broken people. For more information, call 618-627-4651 or visit 3ABN's Web site: www.3ABN.org.

Unless otherwise noted, Scriptures are from The New King James Version, copyright © 1979, 1980, 1982, Thomas Nelson, Inc., Publishers.

Scriptures quoted from TLB are from *The Living Bible*, copyright © 1971 by Tyndale House Publishers, Wheaton, IL. Used by permission.

Scriptures quoted from KJV are from the King James Version.

Scripture quotations marked NIV are from the HOLY BIBLE, NEW INTERNATIONAL VERSION®. Copyright © 1973, 1978, 1984 by International Bible Society. Used by permission of Zondervan Publishing House. All Rights reserved.

Library of Congress Cataloging-in-Publication Data

Kuzma, Kay.
  Serious about love : straight talk to single adults / Kay Kuzma.
    p. cm.
  ISBN 13: 978-0-8163-2338-8 (paper back)
  ISBN 10: 0-8163-2338-0
  1. Man-woman relationships. 2. Dating (Social customs) 3. Mate selection. I. Title.
  HQ801.K889 2009
  248.8'44—dc22

                                                                    2009003124

09 10 11 12 13 • 5 4 3 2 1

DEDICATED TO MY CHILDREN AND THEIR MARRIAGE PARTNERS

Kim and Ed
Kari and Jeff
Kevin and Angela

May you always remember that . . .

"Through wisdom a house is built,
And by understanding it is established;
By knowledge the rooms are filled
With all precious and pleasant riches."

Proverbs 24:3, 4, NKJV

With special thanks to Kari St. Clair for the time, wisdom, and insights
she shared with her mom as she edited this book.
It wouldn't have been the same without her!

CONTENTS

INTRODUCTION

Are you anticipating making an investment in marriage sometime soon? Marriage isn't like the stock market—you don't pick up a good-looking marriage partner and hold on to it as long as it proves to be a good investment and then dump it for another when it starts to slump. Marriage is an investment for life.

You owe it to yourself to find out what it takes to be happy and fulfilled in a lifetime commitment. Do you have the information you need to choose a marriage partner wisely?

You're mature enough to realize that love and marriage aren't necessarily forever. You've watched some of your friends fall in love, marry, and divorce. Others are struggling to hold things together, and many are merely existing as married singles. Or perhaps you've gone through a bad relationship, experienced a traumatic breakup, and want desperately to avoid making the same mistake again! You want something better. Not only do you want to avoid the devastating agony of rejection and divorce, but you also want to experience all that God intended marital love to be.

This book is for those who are serious about love. It is for you who have gone through the teenage turmoil of falling in and out of puppy love and are now seriously searching for a lifetime marriage partner.

Walk as rationally as possible through the dating process. Give yourself time to determine whether you are courting the right mate. There is nothing more bankrupting than making a long-term investment in what turns out to be short-term interest.

Don't give up your idealism. It is possible to have your dreams come true. In spite of difficult days, you can experience a sustaining sense of intimate, unconditional love in your marriage. But don't kid yourself—it won't happen by chance.

Finding the happiness you're looking for depends a great deal on two factors: choosing the right mate and being the right mate for the person you choose. A little advice: choose wisely. Love is not enough to keep a marriage together.

If you are seriously considering marriage, read this book with your loved one. Make a promise to yourself and to each other to evaluate the risk factors for alienation and divorce. Work out major and minor problems in your relationship *before* you marry.

Marriage is a commitment for life. The choices you make before marriage are critical for your future happiness. They help you discover who you are and what makes your heart sing. So live each day to the fullest, becoming the person God wants you to be. Believe that God has good things planned for you and it is His heart's desire to give you your heart's desire. Don't settle for anything less.

—Kay Kuzma

CHAPTER 1

WHAT DO YOU WANT OUT OF MARRIAGE?

A bishop was administering confirmation to a group of young people and asked a nervous child, "How does the catechism define *matrimony*?"

The child hesitated for a moment and then said, "It is a state of terrible torment which those who are compelled to enter undergo for a time to fit them for the better world."

"No, no," interrupted the parish priest. "You've mixed up the definition of *matrimony* with the definition of *purgatory*!"

"Let it be." The bishop smiled. "How do two priests like you and me know that the child is not right?"

Every bride and groom says "I do" with the expectation that their marriage is going to be different. They believe their union will bring true fulfillment and intimacy. A young couple would never walk down the aisle if they knew they were entering a state of "purgatory." People get married because they dream of living happily ever after. They want heaven on earth—not hell!

But so few reach the ideal! Why is that? Is there something you can do to enable your marriage to be everything you hope it will be?

CHOOSING A MARRIAGE PARTNER

Marriage is a pivotal point. In one way or another, everything beyond it will be affected by the one you choose as your mate. Choosing a marriage partner who will stand the test of time is the most important decision you will ever have to make. Yet many people are more serious about checking out the car they want to buy than the person they want to marry. Can you imagine buying a car on feelings alone?

If you want to avoid marital misery, you have to have a goal above and beyond merely finding the person who turns you on. And it's probably not wise to get married just because you've found someone who meets your needs. You must consider every aspect of the other person's life in relationship to your own.

Marriage is a lifelong commitment, regardless of personality, handicaps, temperament, money, looks, or health. This commitment shouldn't be hard to keep. It shouldn't be work! To love your mate as yourself is meant to be the most natural response of your being.

It takes a great deal of effort to have a good marriage, but it doesn't have to be a chore. If you have a job just to get a paycheck, that's work. But if your job is something you would do regardless of the pay, you can give it everything you've got and it wouldn't seem like work at all. Every successful marriage takes effort, but if you marry the right mate for you and you choose to be the right mate for the person you marry, you'll find satisfaction is easier to obtain.

What's the right mate? It's someone who sees your dreams and your potential and helps you pursue them. The right mate encourages you to become the highest version of the grandest vision that you are! Being the right mate means your greatest desire is to do the same for the other.

I believe many marriages end up in a state of terrible torment because people don't know themselves and what makes their hearts sing. They don't have a plan for their lives. Instead, they follow their feelings, make poor choices in the person they date, and then hope their beloved will magically change, become their ideal mate, and bring them lasting fulfillment by meeting all their needs. Let me tell you, that scenario seldom happens.

Avoiding the Less-Than-Ideal Marriage

Before you choose a mate, it is very important to decide what you want out of marriage. You need to know where you're going in order to determine how to get there.

Most people want romance, intimacy, a sense of fulfillment and companionship in a marriage. They want an equal partnership—not a union in which one dominates the other. The ideal marriage is two people continuing to grow in love, understanding, and unity. They are totally committed to explore and rediscover each other as they experience life together, meeting each other's needs regardless of health, wealth, or whether the cap gets put on the toothpaste tube. That's marital bliss.

Most newlyweds start out expecting that theirs will be the ideal marriage. But few retain this expectation past the first five years. The ideal is possible only when the couple commits to and actively works on keeping their marriage vital by encouraging each other's personal growth.

Many marriages simply die after the first few years. The divorce statistics verify this fact. And what happens to the rest? They may survive, but too often they become something less than the ideal. Usually these marriages fall into one of the following categories: a marriage of convenience, a devitalized marriage, a dominant/submissive marriage, or a conflict-filled marriage.

Let's peek at these less-than-ideal marriages. If you don't like what you see and want to avoid them, the rest of this book will help guide you through your dating and courtship period so your marriage can be everything you want it to be. If you date wisely, you will have the best possible chance of experiencing a dynamic marriage in which both partners are committed to growing together in a meaningful, lifelong relationship.

THE CONVENIENT MARRIAGE

A marriage of convenience is like a business partnership. The husband and wife need each other to pay the bills, take care of the kids, entertain, and share the driving on vacations. But as far as the day-to-day routine, there is very little, if any, pizzazz in their relationship. They might consider getting a divorce because marital satisfaction is low, but for the time being, it's just convenient for the kids and each other to stick it out

Jerry and Trish live in a convenient marriage relationship. Jerry is a physician with a life of his own. He needs a wife to take care of things on the home front, and Trish is comfortable to have around. If something ever happened to her, he admits he would get married again.

"Being married solves a lot of problems," he says. "You have someone to talk to, cook meals, do the shopping, entertain guests, and someone to escort to social functions."

And how does Trish feel about her marriage?"

"Well," she says, "it's certainly not the Romeo and Juliet romance I used to fantasize about when I was a kid. I knew my parents had a marriage of convenience—they would have never survived out on the farm without each other—but I never thought my marriage was going to turn out like this.

"It's a stable marriage, though, so I'm a lot better off than many of my friends. I know Jerry needs me to keep things up around the house, but he has his own career and I have mine. I've just recently become the chairperson of the United Way campaign in our district and find myself working almost as hard as Jerry. I have my own friends, and Jerry has his.

"At night it's nice to know there is someone around. It would be terribly lonely living alone now that the kids have left the nest."

This is a typical marriage of convenience. It isn't a bad marriage; it's just not the type most young lovers look forward to.

What causes a marriage to deteriorate into this living arrangement? It may be that the couple did not share the same ideal of what type of marriage they wanted. Or their ideas of marriage may have changed with the reality of daily responsibilities and busy schedules. They may have become so engrossed in the business of taking care of and supporting the children that they neglected their own relationship. They may not have had the communication skills necessary to discuss what was happening to their relationship or the commitment to turn it around. Similar interests that serve to pull a couple together might have been missing. Without these vital ingredients, it's easy for a dynamic honeymoon to disintegrate into a marriage of convenience.

THE DEVITALIZED MARRIAGE

The devitalized marriage starts out with high expectations and a keen sense of romance, but early in the marriage something happens. The couple forgets to continue those early attentions. They may have gotten married in the passion stage of their relationship and exchanged vows before they learned to communicate their needs. They didn't realize the importance of continuing to court each other after the intense feelings of desire mellowed to a stable state of true love. And now they wonder, "Why did we get married?"

More women than men categorize their marriages as devitalized, probably because women tend to entertain romantic fantasies fostered by society and media. And they may not be as fulfilled in their careers as men often are. These women usually get married with the idea that their Prince Charming will continue to sweep them off their feet as he did during their courtship. Unfortunately, many prince charmings tend to perform valiantly only when there is a prize to be won. Once the wedding and honeymoon are over, they move on to other conquests—not women, necessarily, but educational pursuits, career advancements, various leisure-time activities, or the stock market. These men love their wives, but they don't go out of their way to meet their emotional needs, and they don't see the value of spending lots of time together, especially if they have different interests and life objectives.

As men near the midlife crisis years (forty to fifty-five), some wake up to the fact that their marriage is no longer very exciting. Now, having achieved educational, career, athletic, and financial objectives, too many men think their lack of fulfillment stems from having married the wrong woman. Far too many make the classical midlife maneuver: he buys an expensive sports car, divorces wife number one and finds an young attractive woman, who soon becomes wife number two. The problem with this scenario is that five years later, he generally finds himself back in a devitalized marriage!

What does a devitalized marriage look like? Here is what Robin says about her devitalized marriage: "Richard was a real romeo during our courtship. Can you imagine, he even hired a couple of his friends to play their guitars and sing outside my dorm window on my birthday. I was really surprised when he asked me for that first date because he ran around with an entirely different crowd than I did. They were the partying type and enjoyed going to the beach or playing tennis on the weekends rather than attending church and giving some of their time to help others. But when I got to know Richard, I liked him. Though we didn't have too much in common, he added a sparkle to my life. If only he would do that now!

"If you had known Richard back in college, you wouldn't believe the change in him. He's all work and no play, and our marriage has become dull—really dull. With three preschoolers, I have my hands full. On the weekends he often asks me to play tennis with him, but I don't enjoy the game that much and hate to make a fool of myself. Sometimes he suggests going to the beach, but it's a lot of trouble to take three preschoolers anywhere. Personally, I'd rather stay home with a good book.

"I know I've grown a little shabby since I'm home all the time, but if Richard would only bring me a rose, or call me passionately on the phone as he used to do, I'd feel more like going the extra mile to make myself more attractive. As it is now, I doubt if he'd even notice."

Would you like to hear how things are from Richard's perspective?

"Robin was one of the most admired women on campus. She was a school leader and highly involved in church programs. That's why I was so surprised she accepted a date with me when I first asked her. I knew I was going to have to do something different to get her attention. I guess I fell for her because I knew I could get almost any girl on campus, but Robin didn't seem to be interested in me. She was a challenge, and I liked that.

"It wasn't long before we got married, and then everything seemed to change. I was always suggesting we go places and do things, and she preferred to stay home. Reading some religious book was not my idea of a good time, so before long we fell into a pattern of each doing our own thing.

"I never expected marriage to be this way. I dreamed of my wife greeting me at the door and showering me with kisses when I got home after a hard day at work. I dreamed of us walking on the beach hand-in-hand or playing a good game of tennis and later relaxing in the spa. But it's like pulling hair to get Robin to do anything with me. That's why I've sort of given up.

"I guess we are two different people with different expectations and different needs. Marriage certainly isn't what I thought it was going to be."

Both Robin and Richard realize that they have a devitalized marriage, but each seems powerless to make changes. If they had taken more time during their courtship to get deeply acquainted with each other, they might have realized how different their interests were. They could have then made a rational choice and a plan of action. "Are our differences too great to get married, or do we have what it takes to make this marriage work? If so, what are we going to do if our relationship starts to deteriorate?"

THE DOMINANT/SUBMISSIVE MARRIAGE

We laugh about the husband being the head of the family and the wife being the neck that turns the head. We make fun of henpecked husbands. We tell jokes about weak men, like the day all the men who wanted to get into heaven were asked to line up behind two signs: one read, "Supreme head of the household," and the other, "Attempted head of the household." All the men lined up in front of the "Attempted head" sign except one man. The others were surprised to see the man in the "Supreme head" line, when they knew how important honesty was in order to get into heaven. Finally, one of the men got up nerve to go over to the man and ask him why he was standing in that line. "Oh," replied the man, "my wife told me to stand here."

In addition to jokes, research doesn't have kind things to say about women who rule the house and treat their husbands in a demeaning way. Strong mothers and weak fathers have even been associated with children, especially sons, choosing the homosexual lifestyle.

While it is fairly plain to see that a dominant wife is not good in a marriage, what about a dominant husband? Here are some examples:

Elly had been married to Al for twelve years. The children were now in school, and she had a great desire to go back and finish her education. But Al refused to let her. He felt it would be a strain on the family finances, and he didn't see the reason she needed to finish since he was willing to support the family.

Char read every marriage book that came along and took every family-related seminar. Her greatest desire was to be the best wife and mother in the world. She tried to share her findings with Bill, but he wouldn't listen. "That new-fangled psychology will just get you into trouble," was his response. Char began to feel that she was always the one who was molding to accommodate Bill's wants and wishes, while Bill had no interest in changing.

Dan kept a tight accounting of the finances, giving Bonnie a weekly allowance for food and supplies. At the end of the week Bonnie had to account for every penny. She couldn't even get herself a candy bar without reporting to Dan.

Missy wouldn't make any decision unless she asked Ted. Whenever the kids asked her for favors, Missy would automatically say, "Ask your father." Ted was the final authority in everything. Missy would always say to her friends, "I wanted to call you last night, but Ted said it was too late," or "I would love to attend your weekly Bible study, but Ted thinks I spend too much time away from the house as it is," or "I love chocolate, but Ted won't let me eat it."

Keith didn't want to be the supreme head of the family, but after Lynn attended a seminar on how to be a good Christian wife, she deferred all the household decisions to him. "Honey, I would like to hang a picture in the living room, but I want to make sure you approve." "Lacey is feeling a little sick today. Do you think I should keep her home?" "Is it OK if I buy some fabric to make myself a dress? Should I get blue or red?" "Do you want to sign Jeff's report card, or should I?" Before marriage Lynn seemed quite capable of making good decisions on her own—that's why Keith married her. Now her submissiveness was driving him up a wall.

Many Christian young people have been conditioned to think that husbands should be the head of the family, but no one would want to find themselves in any of these controlling situations. The ideal solution is to recognize God as the head of the family, and side-by-side the husband and wife lead in the family's daily affairs in areas where each is most competent.

Then what do you do with the biblical counsel in Ephesians 5 that says wives should submit to their husbands? Notice it follows the counsel in verse 21 that both husband and wife should submit to each other. This is God's ideal. Occasionally, however, if a couple can't seem to agree on a solution, then God instructed wives to submit rather than fight. It's healthy advice. It keep wives from becoming so dominate that to keep peace husbands have no choice but to give in. Women seldom respect weak men—or dominant ones! Instead of being other-oriented, which is the basis of a healthy marriage, dominance is self-oriented. It's selfish to want your way above the wishes or wants of your spouse. And it's certainly not God's ideal.

God did not create Adam to be Eve's superior, or Eve to be Adam's. He created them to be different, each to enhance the other for perfect fulfillment, but equal in value. If God created Eve from a piece of Adam's brain or from his foot, we might conclude that superiority was a part of God's plan. But God didn't do that. Instead, God used Adam's rib. How symbolic of the fact that husband and wife should stand together side by side as equally valuable partners in a lifelong commitment to each other.

What kind of a marriage do you want? When it comes to practical daily living and marriage satisfaction, most lovers want a marriage in which both love and respect each other so much that dominance is not an issue.

THE CONFLICT-FILLED MARRIAGE

A conflict-dominated marriage occurs when each partner is convinced of his or her infallibility and becomes rigid and defensive. Neither one sees a need to learn the art of negotiation. The prevailing attitude is, Why compromise when your opinion is right?

Before marriage, because each is trying so hard to please the other, it is sometimes difficult to determine just how prone a couple might be to experience a conflict-filled marriage someday. Ideally, this wanting-to-please-each-other behavior should continue throughout marriage, but sometimes it doesn't. Instead, after marriage, each feels freer to express an opinion without regard for how it might make the other person feel. In a good marriage, where each respects the other, the free expression of personal opinions is healthy. But where there isn't much respect, too often the conflict results in hostility. When this happens, the time the couple could spend enjoying the other is eaten away in senseless battles.

Why don't these couples get a divorce? As one woman said, "If we get a divorce, who would we have to argue with?" One husband commented, "I would never let myself become involved in this type of arguing in any other relationship, but it just seems the thing to do with my wife."

God designed the marriage institution to provide a safe climate for growth and change. Marriage is meant to be an ideal relationship in which each partner is nurtured and supported in such a way as to increase both individual and couple potential. The effect of living in a conflict-filled marriage is exactly the opposite: it stifles growth and improvement. It breaks the other down instead of building him or her up. In addition, hostile words dishonor God (Matthew 5:21, 22). As long as the devil can keep a couple arguing, their marriage will be a state of terrible torment, regardless of whether or not they consider divorce.

How can you determine if your relationship is heading toward a conflict-filled marriage? Watch for signs of nagging, bossiness, or any other behavior you find irritating. It's possible to be so infatuated that you overlook negative behavior patterns or think that these will be overcome with love. Unfortunately, after marriage, when the relationship is secure and the realization begins to dawn that this undesirable behavior is increasing instead of decreasing, the previously docile partner is likely to begin standing up for his or her rights. The result? More conflict.

Danielle was a born leader. She was outgoing, talkative, decisive, and quick to point out what needed to be done in order to solve a problem. She respected people who were experts in their fields and often criticized those who weren't. She married Travis. He thought carefully before speaking, took his time to get things done, and would never think of pushing others or himself. He may have appeared on the outside to be fairly compliant because of his quiet ways, but he had a strong mind of his own.

Things went well until the faucet started leaking and the house needed painting. "Travis, do you know how many gallons of water we are wasting with that leaky faucet?" Danielle asked. "It's got to be fixed this weekend."

But Travis was in the middle of a book and read the weekend away.

"Travis, I can't stand this peeling paint." Danielle complained. "Either you get this house scraped and painted, or I'll use our vacation money and have a professional painter do it."

Travis calmly stated, "I'll do it." And he was going to, but he wasn't about to miss a finance seminar that was going on that week. Two months later the faucet still leaked and the paint on the house was still peeling.

Danielle grew more disturbed. Why couldn't Travis be more like her father, who was interested in keeping things in good repair around the home? Travis was so clumsy when it came to practical things like fixing the toaster or putting up wallpaper. (She hadn't noticed this before marriage.) The more she criticized him, the more her respect for him dropped—and the more biting her tongue became.

For seven years Travis calmly took this abuse, and then one day he stood up to her. His pent-up hostility caused him to say hurtful, mean things in front of the children. He had lost respect for his wife and treated her accordingly.

Chances are Danielle and Travis never understood the practical meaning of *respect.* If you respect another person, you will not nag or boss, even if your natural self feels like it. You will check your words, making sure they uplift and instruct rather than tear down.

If Danielle and Travis hadn't rushed into marriage, these obnoxious, conflict-causing traits probably would have surfaced before their wedding date, and they would have made a more informed choice.

If you want to avoid a conflict-filled marriage, give yourselves the time you need to analyze carefully every noticeable trait about each other—especially the negative ones. Ask yourself, "Can I learn to love and respect a spouse with that trait?" Even though you feel it's negative, could it be viewed as positive because it would encourage your own personal growth? Take time to discuss the behavior that bothers you. There's a lot more motivation for changing traits before marriage than after! For those traits where change is highly unlikely, discuss how these might affect your marriage. While it's impossible to anticipate everything that might surface in your marriage, the more potential problems you recognize and deal with before the wedding date, the fewer the heartbreaking surprises afterward.

THE UNIQUELY COMPLEMENTARY MARRIAGE

You've just read about some less-than-ideal marriage models, and ideally you've made a strong decision that you don't want any of those. Now it's time to set your sights on what God wants for you to experience in this most wonderful relationship that He has created. I call this type of marriage "uniquely complementary."

Men and women are different. That's the way God created them. The deepest need for a man is to be masculine and for a woman, to be feminine. Not only are their bodies different, but the core longings of their souls are different.

Men and women may have the same careers, face the same challenges in their families, and develop the same skills and abilities, but they find meaning and fulfillment in different ways.

Carol Gilligan's research, reported in her book *In a Different Voice,*[1] found that a man sees himself as competent and mature when he can move into his world as a complete and separate individual. He feels successful when he is free to make his own decisions and feel a sense of security within himself. In contrast, a woman finds meaning and fulfillment in nurturing and experiencing close and warm relationships with people, especially her family and friends. This doesn't mean that she doesn't enjoy having a fulfilling career. It just means that career is not usually of ultimate importance to a woman's sense of being.

Here's the good news: God created man to meet his wife's deepest yearning for relationship. And at the same time, God created woman to meet her husband's deepest yearning for affirmation as he moves purposefully into his world. That's why the apostle Paul spent eleven verses in Ephesians 5 (verses 23–33) telling men how to love their wives, and two verses (verses 24 and 33) telling wives how to respect their husbands. If a man, as spiritual head or leader of the family, will meet his wife's relational and emotional needs (similar to how Christ meets our needs), it follows that she will respect and admire him.

It was God's design that a husband and a wife would fit together perfectly, both physically as well as emotionally. Each was made to supply the needs of the other. They were created to be complementary. They were made to "serve one another in love," as the apostle Paul admonishes us to do in Galatians 5:13, NIV.

In a way, there is no such thing as a marriage model that neatly fits every couple. It's impossible to say, "If men would just be breadwinners and women bread-makers, all marital difficulties would be solved." Marital bliss has little to do with the fulfillment of specific tasks or roles. It has everything to do with the fulfillment of each other's emotional needs.

Because each individual is unique, *each couple has a unique fit that is suitable only for them.* Larry Crabb, author of *Men and Women: Enjoying the Difference,*[2] says that God gives each couple the happy task of discovering and delighting in this unique fit.

So the question remains, *What do you want out of marriage?* If you want a dynamic uniquely complementary marriage with your love for each other growing stronger and more intimate each passing year, then it becomes absolutely essential that throughout your courtship you continually assess whether you are dating the right mate—and whether you are the right mate for the person you are dating.

SOMETHING TO THINK ABOUT . . .

- What do you want out of marriage? Take some time to write down your answer.
- If you are seriously dating someone, discuss your expectations of marriage with each other.
  - ○ In what ways do you agree?
  - ○ How do you disagree?
  - ○ Are your disagreements signaling potential problem areas? If so, what?
  - ○ Discuss what you can do now to solve problems rather than wait until they negatively impact your relationship.

---

1. Carol Gilligan, *In a Different Voice* (Boston, Mass.: Harvard University Press, 1982), 159–163.

2. Larry Crabb, *Men and Women: Enjoying the Difference* (Grand Rapids, Mich.: Zondervan Publishing House, 1991).

CHAPTER 2:
DATE THE RIGHT MATE OR BEWARE OF YOUR FATE

It's easy to fall in love. Maybe it's the beauty queen, the soccer hero, the straight-A student, the class president, or the most talented member of the art club. Something about this person captivates your thoughts and melts your heart. We call it love, but it's not lasting. The fact is people fall in love many times before they are really serious about love—often with individuals who would make very poor marriage partners. Obviously you won't marry everyone you fall in love with, but the chances are quite high that you will promise to love, honor, and obey someone you will date in the next few years.

Too many people say, "I do," in the heat of romance, only to discover that hot summer love isn't necessarily rational. *It is possible to be madly in love with the wrong person. And being in love is not reason enough to marry.* Marriages based on love alone may make it through the fall of a relationship as passion begins to cool, but when love settles down for a long winter's night—and rationality returns—too many discover that they have made a long-term investment in a short-term interest.

Have you ever heard someone say after the first date or two, "I could never fall in love with him!" or "She's not my type." But if they continue to date, or just have long talks, e-mail, text, and spend time together because there's no one else more interesting, too often they are sending out wedding invitations six months later.

Beware! Your emotions can play tricks on you. No matter what you may tell yourself, given the right conditions, you can fall in love with almost anyone. And it all starts with that first date. That's why it is very important to assess the person you continue to date to make sure he or she has the characteristics you want in a mate.

There are two types of dating, but the line between them is not always easy to distinguish. Friendship or casual dating is when you are just interested in making new friends and finding out how it feels to be with certain people. You enjoy group gatherings, or you might do lunch or study together. This is discovery dating. You are basically saying to the other person, "I'd like to get to know you. I'd like to experience what it's like to hang out with you. Let's see what works and what doesn't." This is the stage where you learn what makes you feel good and what doesn't. If a date has certain traits that you admire, put those traits on a list of what you want in a mate. If nothing clicks, thank the person for letting you experience who you are *not*, and move on. When you're friendship dating, you have little desire to continue going with the same individual on a long-term basis.

Serious dating is where you desire to continue the dating relationship to see if you have long-term compatibility. Whether you admit it or not, you are searching for someone you'd like to marry. You now know the person well enough to think this might be it.

When you move to serious dating, be honest with each other. "I want to get to know you better because you have many characteristics that I admire and would like to have in a mate someday. If it works, great! If not, let's thank each other for some good times and fun memories, and move on."

Because these two types of dating are so closely related, and can quickly move from one stage to another, it is important that you spend as much time as possible with a group of friends, so you can be as selective as possible when you begin pairing off.

LEARNING TO DETERMINE WHO'S RIGHT FOR YOU

How can you determine who is the right date for you? That's complicated because each person's strengths and weaknesses, family and cultural background, interests, talents, intellect, and ambitions are different. But regardless of personal preference, you'll want to stay away from the situation Larry got himself into.

I know Larry well. When he went to college, he wasn't interested in getting serious. He wanted to date young women who didn't have marriage on their minds. That's why he was so pleased when he met Kathy. She was good looking and dating a guy back home, so they could have a good time together, and he wouldn't have to worry about her getting serious. Since it was not much fun to go places alone, this arrangement was convenient for both of them.

But the more time they spent together, the more they enjoyed it. Then summer came and Kathy went back to her old boyfriend, Joe. When school started again, Larry and Kathy took up where they had left off—and their relationship grew without their realizing what was happening. Six months later Kathy broke up with Joe. Kathy and Larry's relationship grew more serious.

Yet something bothered Larry. He had made a list of the characteristics he wanted to have in a future wife, and there were a number of traits Kathy didn't have. He was especially worried about Kathy's emotional instability. Should he keep the relationship going, or should he break up? He took his problem to the Lord.

One night after agonizing over this situation, Larry opened his Bible, and his eyes focused on Isaiah 62:5: "And as the bridegroom rejoices over the bride, / So shall your God rejoice over you." He took this as an answer to his prayer, an assurance from the Lord that it was OK to continue dating Kathy.

Their relationship advanced, but every time Kathy went back home and saw Joe, she became confused. She eventually broke up with Larry, but after two weeks she couldn't stand it and begged him to take her back. He did, thinking that finding the Bible text was God's assurance that Kathy would someday be his.

Larry and Kathy became engaged. Then summer came, and when Kathy once again saw Joe, she was torn. At the end of the summer she broke her engagement to Larry and within months married Joe. Larry was devastated. Had God failed him?

Later, after Larry fell in love with and married a woman with whom he had more in common and who more closely met his criteria for an ideal wife, he looked back and realized that marrying Kathy would have been a mistake. Her emotional instability would have been like a noose around his neck, zapping all his emotional energy in trying to meet her needs.

There is a triple moral to this true story.

1. Don't steadily date someone just because you're lonely or you don't think you could get serious—unless that person truly is the kind of person you would want to marry someday. It's easy to con yourself into thinking nothing will come of your friendship because the person you are dating is more like a buddy than a girlfriend or boyfriend. But that's not necessarily true. Old flames do die, and bonding happens when you spend time together regardless of whether you feel the person has good marriage potential.

2. Don't fall into the trap of putting a fleece before the Lord or claiming a Bible verse to make the decision of a marriage partner for you. God has given you a mind, adequate information, parental counsel, and professional help so you can make an intelligent decision. Use them.

3. *Don't marry someone who is double bonded or still in love with another.* In other words, don't get married if either one of you has recently broken up with someone else. It takes time to become emotionally detached from a close, long-term, intimate relationship. Kathy never did and Larry suffered because of it. Time is a wonderful healer, but you've got to give it a chance to do its work.

BEWARE OF BEING "NEEDED"

There are dangers in dating someone who needs you is another moral too many couples become aware of too late. It's nice to feel needed, but overdependence doesn't wear well in a marriage relationship. Two happy people usually make a happy marriage. Two needy ones make a needy marriage—one that has more needs than the couple is able to fulfill.

John and Phyllis were in my husband's class in college. Phyllis had come from an abusive home. She was defensive and cold, and she harbored internal anger. John was a good listener, and Phyllis needed a counselor. John spent hours listening to the sordid story of Phyllis's past. He tried to give her the kind of encouragement she needed to get out of the psychological low she was in. His friends, including my husband, couldn't understand why John was investing so much time in Phyllis. They warned him, but he merely laughed at their concern. A year later John and Phyllis got engaged. They married, had two children, and divorced after seven years.

No one wants to be married to a counselee. It just doesn't work. It's easy for the counselor to get tired of continually being responsible for someone else's happiness or to feel rejected when he is no longer needed. And on the other head, who wants to be married to a lifetime counselor?

How much better it would be to seek professional counseling before marriage so you can enter into a relationship without needless emotional baggage. The best marriage partners are those who have solved personal problems before the wedding ceremony so they can concentrate on giving love to the other rather than selfishly seeing how much they can get.

WHAT YOU CAN (AND CANNOT) CHANGE

A final moral to consider: *you can't change anyone unless he or she wants to change.* It's foolish to think that your efforts alone will make the man or woman you are dating into a significantly different person. Change happens when people feel a need for change and recognize that if they don't change, they'll experience negative consequences. When the perceived benefit from change is great enough, change is more likely.

Tony was in danger of flunking calculus when he met Tammy, an honor student. Because Tony was a strong, handsome, likeable guy, who enjoyed having a good time, Tammy was thrilled when he started paying attention to her. She respected his athletic ability, and in spite of his low grades, he seemed intelligent and talked of graduate school. He blamed his grades and low GPA on his lack of interest and his desire to enjoy life.

Tammy began tutoring Tony in calculus, which meant they spent many hours together in his apartment. The more time they spent together, the more their feelings for each other grew. Tammy was already madly in love with Tony when it dawned on her that Tony wasn't really as interested in intellectual pursuits as she was. In fact, he probably would never go to graduate school. But she kidded herself into believing that if she could only help him enough, he would change.

Ten years after they were married, Tony was quite comfortable spending his leisure time having fun, watching TV, and reading the sports section of the paper, while Tammy felt her intellectual self—and her respect for Tony—dying. She admired the sharp intellectual businessmen she worked with, and she found it difficult not to compare them to her husband. In addition, she resented Tony for not encouraging her to pursue her own educational goals.

More and more she entertained the thought, *Would my dream of getting a PhD destroy my marriage by creating an even larger intellectual gap between us? If only . . .*

Deep down we all want to be loved unconditionally for who we are. It's unfair to expect major changes from someone who has not given any indication that he or she plans on being any different. Had Tammy looked at her relationship with Tony honestly, she probably would have made a different decision about their marriage. Perhaps she would have looked for someone who not only was fun to be with, but also enjoyed educational excellence and inspired her to fulfill her own dreams.

In summary, don't steadily date someone who is not the type of person you want to marry. Basically, don't marry someone . . .

on blind faith;

who is double bonded;

who is your counselor or counselee;

who is overly dependent on you (or mom or dad) to meet his or her needs;

or who has unresolved problems of the past;

and don't marry someone whom you think you can change.

All of these morals tell us one thing: *beware of dating yourself into a lopsided love relationship.* Remember the biblical counsel not to be unequally yoked together (2 Corinthians 6:14)? Could this instruction be broadly applied beyond the usual interpretation of unequal yoking of believers with unbelievers? True love blossoms best in a balanced relationship. It brings a sense of freedom to each partner. With each other's encouragement and support, you can be everything God intended you to be.

SPECIAL DATING SITUATIONS

In the world of young-adult dating, you will find individuals who have been previously married and either divorced or widowed, and they may or may not have children. Any time you date someone who was previously married, you face special issues. It doesn't mean that person wouldn't make an ideal mate, but you need to be aware of factors that may complicate life and may pose some major challenges. You are not just marrying the person, you are marrying his or her past. Can you handle it? Is your character up to it?

To help you determine whether pursuing a relationship with a previously married person is right for you, here are some questions to ask:

DATING A WIDOW OR WIDOWER

1. Is the person ready to move on to a new relationship? How long has it been since the death? How did the person die? Has he or she grieved sufficiently to bury the past?

2. Is the person able to move on to a new relationship and not compare you to the old? Love the second time around will be different. Is the person willing to embrace the newness of your relationship and let go of the old?

3. Is the family of the first spouse so wrapped up in the life of the person you're dating, that they will be part of the marriage package? *Just because their adult child has died, doesn't mean that they should be expected to give up a meaningful relationship with their previous son- or daughter-in-law.*

4. Relationships are further complicated if there are children involved. The dead person's parents will always be grandma and grandpa to the children. Can you live with an extra set of parents: yours, your mates, and your mate's previous in-laws?

5. Are you going to be expected to live in the same house as the person you're dating and the first spouse lived in? How many of the previous spouse's possessions are going to be brought into your home?

6. Are you able to talk with your date about the person who died, see pictures of the person you're dating with the previous spouse, and hear family talk about old family memories without feeling jealous?

DATING A DIVORCEE

Dating someone who has been divorced is risky. Here's why: (1) A person with a history of a failed marriage probably has emotional baggage that could affect your marriage. (2) Divorced individuals, when they remarry, find it easier to divorce a second time. It often becomes their way of solving marital problems. However, if a person has learned valuable lessons from experiencing a divorce, the person may be a stronger, more accepting, and more dedicated marriage partner. The important thing to remember is that you don't want to have to compete with the past. This is a new relationship. You chose each other. Embrace that fact and move on. Here are some questions you'll want to ask to help determine if this individual is right for you—and whether you are right for the other.

1. Is the person's divorce final? Have all the assets been distributed? How long has it been final? *You'll have a better chance for a successful marriage, if you don't have to be involved in settlements that have to do with the past.*

2. How accepting is your own family to the idea that you are dating and may marry a divorced person? How accepting are your friends?

3. Have you been able to talk openly about your date's previous marriage and what happened? Have you been able to talk to his or her ex to get the rest of the story?

4. Is your date willing to take part of the responsibility for the failed marriage, or is it always the other person's fault? *If he or she blames the other, the chances are great that the person may have difficulty admitting mistakes.*

5. What has this person learned from the divorce so this mistake won't be repeated again?

6. What is this person going to do differently if married to you in order to ensure a lifelong relationship?

7. Is alimony being paid to the ex? What about child support? If payments are to be made, how much? Is it possible to have the financial advantages you want in a marriage when this amount is going to support a previous family? Is this person current on alimony or child-support payments?

8. Will the ex be a part of your lives? Is he or she still in phone or e-mail contact? How often do they see each other? What issues do they discuss? Is their relationship really over? *Note: if they have children, it will never be over.* Are you prepared to share your spouse with his or her ex? What boundaries does the person you're dating plan to set so the past doesn't interfere with the present?

9. Is this person willing to move slowly through the friendship and casual dating stages in your dating relationship so that your relationship is based on a solid friendship? Is he or she willing to make a marriage commitment and wait until marriage for sex? *Most divorced individuals tend to be more open to a sexual relationship before marriage, or they tend to marry quite quickly after the divorce. Or it could be that the person is so gun-shy about marriage that he or she is afraid to make another commitment and just wants a good steady friend.*

10. If children are involved, who are the children living with? Is the person you're dating really wanting a marriage partner, or is the primary goal to have someone to help take care of the children or to be a good role model for the missing parent? Are the children living with the person you're marrying? If so, how well do you like the kids? Are you ready to be a parent on the day you wed? Have the children fully accepted you? *If not, don't get married yet. Children of divorced parents often have a fantasy that their parents will remarry, as in the classic film* The Parent Trap. *If you come into the picture, you destroy their dream, and they can*

retaliate in such a way as to make life miserable for you. Let marriage wait until you win them over, or as some individuals have done, until the kids leave the nest! But even then, grown kids can be so jealous and vindictive, that they may never truly accept you. Can you live with that?

11. If there is split custody, or if primary custody is with the other parent, are you ready to have these children come in and out of your life—for the rest of your life? How well do you like the children? Do they like you? If something would happen to the ex who now has custody, would the children come to live full time with you? Is this something that you could handle?

12. Have you considered having your own children once married? *If so, the problems of his kids, her kids, and our kids can be quite a challenge.* Are you ready for that?

13. Is this person wanting to have any more children? If not, what does that do to your dream to have your own children? Can you live with that decision?

DATING SOMEONE WITH CHILDREN

If the person you are dating has kids, here is the principle to follow to determine whether or not you should pursue this relationship. *If you're not madly in love with the kids, and don't feel you would be an incredible parent—as well as an excellent spouse—it's NOT fair to the children for you to become involved in their lives.* It's not their fault that they lost a parent. It hurts badly enough to feel the loss and rejection from death or divorce. The last thing they need is for someone to come into their lives, steal their surviving parent's affection, and treat them like second-class citizens. Please don't do that! So, here's your checklist:

1. Have I spent enough time with the kids to grow to love them supremely and unconditionally?
2. Are these the children I want to be in my life forever?
3. Do I have adequate parenting skills to take on the parenting job?
4. Do the children respect me enough to obey me? Will I be able to effectively discipline them?
5. Do I agree with the parenting style of the person I'm dating?
6. Are my parents ready to be grandparents to children that weren't born to me?

7. Do I feel I have the patience, skills, and time necessary to help the kids work through their problems? If not, what am I willing to do to get them the help they need?

8. Am I willing to go to counseling if one or more of the children is having difficulties? Am I willing to spend money on counseling, or will I resent how much the children are costing? *Remember, children of divorce or death must deal with major issues of rejection and loss. They have been severely hurt. If you marry a person with challenging children, those challenges immediately become yours.*

9. If you have children, ask: How will this marriage affect my own children? Is marriage the best thing I can do for my children at this time of their lives? Does the person I'm dating have the qualities I want my children to model?

DANGEROUS DATING

Not only do you want to find and date the right mate, but you want to make sure you avoid a dangerous one. There are many hidden hazards in the world of dating. Even though you're still in the friendship stage of a relationship, or just casually dating around, it is important to be aware of putting yourself in unsafe situations. Not every person is what they appear to be at first—or second—meeting. Not every person has pure motives for wanting to get to know you, and, therefore, when someone asks for your phone number or address, be cautious about giving it out.

If you associate mainly with Christians, you might think that you don't have to worry about your safety. The sad truth is that not every Christian has Christian intentions about what they want out of a relationship. That's why I end this chapter with some red flags for you to watch out for in your dating relationships. Armed with this information, you will be better able to protect yourself.

INTERNET DATING

Many young people are joining Internet dating services or chat rooms to see who's out there. Since they haven't yet found a compatible date among their peers, they are curious to see who the computer will match them with. Online dating has become an accepted way of finding a great mate, but it's not without some major hazards.

How do you know which dating service is right for you? Many are free, but most have a membership fee, especially if they offer matches based on sophisticated personality profiles and important variables such as religion, hobbies, and interests. Many church denominations have their own online services. That's a good place to start, as long as the data base is sufficient to find adequate matches. Next, check out the services that will match you on religious background as well as a detailed personality profile. Finally, ask yourself: Do I want a long-distance relationship? Am I willing to move? If not, check out dating services that match on religion and location.

Once you have submitted your profile, it will take time to sort through the matches you're likely to get. In the process, remember that the anonymity of internet dating has opened up a new playground for con artists. Dishonest people can present themselves as the person they think you're looking for, rather than showing their true colors. Believe it or not, it's easy to fall in love over the Internet because of the high degree of anticipation, fantasy, and sense of adventure. By the time you begin to suspect that you're dealing with a dishonest person, you may be so emotionally attached that you throw reason to the wind, deny the truth, and continue your nightly "dates" in the chat room. So here are the red flags you'll want to look out for.

1. *Don't be gullible.* Internet dating is one of the easiest places for someone to cheat on their spouse or the person they're seriously dating or engaged to. All a person has to do is get a secret e-mail address, create a persona, use a cell phone, and have mail sent to a post office box. Don't be too trusting. When a person doesn't want you to call during evenings and weekends, or if after a reasonable time, the person won't give you a home phone number, that's a major red flag. If you begin to suspect the person is telling "white" lies, ask straight out about his or her living arrangement. Is he living with someone or married? Does she have children? If a person lies in the beginning of a relationship, don't kid yourself into believing the person will miraculously change.

2. *When you're first getting acquainted, don't be too specific about giving out identity information.* There are predators and stalkers out there. When

asked where you live, give the county, not the exact city or street. If they ask for your phone number, ask for their number first and say you'll call them—and make sure you can't be identified by caller ID.

3. *Be careful in sending out photos.* Once you do, that person can do anything with them. Your image is part of your identity, so protect it. But at the same time, once you get acquainted, ask the other person for a few recent photographs. Sometimes the one posted on the Internet is computer enhanced—or was taken a number of years ago.

4. *Don't disclose what you possess—or how rich your dad is!* Be careful about giving information about how much you have in the bank, what real estate you own, and what kind of a car you drive. You don't want someone more interested in your possessions than in you.

5. *Ask for references.* Once you become interested in this person, it's not unreasonable to ask for three or four names and numbers of individuals who are willing to talk to you about the person's personality and character. If the person has nothing to hide, this shouldn't be a problem. If religion is important to you, make sure at least one of the references is a pastor and/or some other professional person who goes to the same church. Beware of getting just a list of friends! And it's always better to actually talk with these individuals, then to e-mail.

6. *After becoming acquainted, ask the other person to remove their Internet profiles and listings.* If they don't want to, that's a sign that they are really not that interested in you.

7. *After a reasonable amount of time, you'll want to actually meet this person you've been chatting with.* It's possible to fall in love with pretty words and flowery phrases, and when you meet the writer to realize that the person is not at all who you expected. So as you plan that first meeting, here are some safety guidelines to follow:

- Meet during the day.

- Meet in a public place surrounded by other individuals, preferably family and friends.
- Don't get into his or her car alone unless you have carefully checked out the person's character and are convinced you'll be safe. Always tell someone where you're going and what time you'll be back. Don't let your emotions or the fantasy of this meeting allow you to get caught in a potentially dangerous situation.
- Don't let yourself get talked into something you don't want to do. Listen to your gut. If this is to be a long-term interest, you will have time for your relationship to advance through the friendship stage before you get physically involved.
- Just in case the person isn't who you were expecting, plan an exit strategy so you won't have to spend a lot of time together. Make the first date a short one. Go someplace you will enjoy regardless of who you are with. Don't lead the person on. If after the first meeting you definitely are not interested in further contact, tell the person it's not going to work. And if there was an expense in setting up this meeting, offer to pay half of it.

Avoiding Date Rape

Although men are sometimes raped, the vast majority of rape victims are women. So women, listen up! Most rape victims are acquainted with their rapist. Date rape is a very real danger. You may think you're just going out for a good time and will be with a group of safe friends, but even a seemingly innocent gathering can prove dangerous. Here are some precautions. Take them seriously or you could be the next victim.

1. *Before you date anyone, invite the person to meet your family and friends— especially older respected friends like a teacher or preacher.* If the person is hesitant to meet these people, it could mean that his dating intentions are questionable. You may think the guy is a great catch, but family and friends might pick up warning signals that you have missed. Take their concerns seriously.

2. *Check out a potential date carefully before saying Yes to going out.* Where does he come from? What is he doing now? Consider his friends. Do

you feel comfortable with them? If your family isn't around to meet your date, suggest that you go to church for your first date.

3. *Don't dress provocatively.* It's very easy for a guy to get the wrong idea about a girl and what she wants on a date by the way she dresses. Remember, men are sexually stimulated by what they see. Just because an outfit is fashionable, doesn't make it safe. If you have questions, ask a trustworthy guy friend. If he thinks it's provocative—don't wear it!

4. *Beware of sending the wrong signals.* Flirting, suggestive body signals, kissing, and caressing tell a man you're interested in sex. You don't have to make out just because your date wants to. Determine what standards you want to live by before walking out the door. Then if he comes on to you, make it clear you won't go there! Just say no, No, NO! And say it early in the game. Explain you don't believe in kissing or making out with guys you don't know well enough to consider them marriage potential! If making out is the only thing he's interested in, ask him to take you home.

5. *Don't go anyplace with someone you have doubts about, especially if you're alone.* Don't date anyone who has a history of having sex with others, even though the person claims he has changed.

6. *Don't double date with a couple you know is having sex.*

7. *Don't go to a party or informal gathering where there are more men than women.*

8. *Be careful about dating older, experienced men.* Don't attend parties where most of the men are older.

9. *Don't go to parties where there may be alcohol, drugs, or questionable activities.*

10. *Tell someone where you are going, with whom, and when you'll return—and let your date know you've done this.*

11. *If you're at a party or group function, call someone to come get you rather accepting a ride home with someone whose intentions or integrity you question.* Never go out without a cell phone and enough money to call a cab in case you need a safe ride home.

12. *Don't allow your date to park in some lonely place, to take you for a walk in a desolate area, or to entice you to come in to see his place if he lives alone.*

13. *Don't believe these come-ons:*

    - "If you love me, you'll let me."
    - "You're so beautiful I can't take my eyes off you."
    - "Everybody's doing it."
    - "I want to show you how much I love you."
    - "What's the matter with you? Are you frigid?"

    A quick comeback, especially one filled with humor, may break the tension and halt the sexual advance.

    - "If you love me, you won't ask me!"
    - "Thank you for the compliment. I can't take my eyes off the refrigerator. Let's get something to eat."
    - "If everybody's doing it, then it should be easy to find someone else."
    - "Instead of showing me how much you love me, why not put it in words."
    - "I am a little cold. I'll go get a sweater."

14. *If you don't have good vibes about a person, don't date.* God gave you your senses to be an early warning system. If you don't feel quite right, don't give out your contact information and make it clear that you're not interested. Or if you're on a date and you begin to feel uncomfortable, be confident in who you are. Stand straight; look the person in the eyes, and say firmly, "No thanks. I'm not interested."

Red Flags to a Potentially Abusive Relationship

Domestic violence often starts in a dating relationship. Many young adults put up with an occasional slap, jabs in the ribs, powerful grips that leave finger-print bruises, and verbal put-downs because they have the mistaken notion that to be loved they must endure pain. This is not true! Abuse should never be a part of a dating relationship—or any other relationship!

Men and women are both at risk for abuse. But many aren't aware of the beginning signs and put up with hurtful behavior thinking that if they can just make the person love them enough, this will stop. On the contrary, if you suf-fer abuse during dating, it will only get worse as you get more involved. So beware of the following red flags.

1. Obsessive jealousy. If your date wants to be with you constantly and ques-tions you about other relationships, it could be a sign of pathological jealousy. The person may even stalk you, call you repeatedly, check on your car mileage, or ask his friends to check on you.

2. Controlling behavior. Sometimes abusers pretend to be concerned for your safety when you're late or when they don't like you doing things on your own—such as going someplace without asking. If someone constantly ques-tions you about how you spend your time, who you see, talk to, or e-mail, what you did or wore and where you went, or requires you to ask permission to do certain things, that's pathological control. Don't let a person trick you into believing that they will "die" without you. And beware of the ultimate control tactic: to threaten suicide if you break up.

3. Unrealistic Expectations. Sometimes abusers compliment you in a way that makes you feel superhuman, or they expect you to be perfect and then trash you when you're not. Beware of the person who is very dependent on you and says things like, "I am all you need. You are all I need."

4. Isolation. Abusers often try to isolate the person they're dating from fam-ily, friends, coworkers, and resources. They may even refuse to let you use your car, talk to others on the phone, or allow you to visit Internet chat rooms.

5. Blames you and others for problems. The abuser is never at fault. Instead, it's always your fault if something goes wrong in the relationship. They say things like, "You made me mad." "You're hurting me by not doing what I ask."

"I can't help being angry." "You control how I feel." In addition, they often deny ever being abusive to anyone else. Their comeback is, "I was only reacting to the other person's abusive behavior."

6. Hypersensitivity. The hypersensitive person is easily insulted and sees everything as a personal attack. He or she looks for fights and blows things out of proportion.

7. Shows disrespect and cruelty to people (especially children) and animals. Beware of the person who treats others in a demeaning and painful manner by teasing, punishing, or tormenting them until they cry or negatively react.

8. Rigid rules about gender. Abusive people can be highly opinionated and extremely rigid. For example, they often believe women are inferior to men, and that there are certain things that are women's work, like changing diapers or cleaning toilets, that men should never do.

9. Sudden mood changes. Abusers sometimes have bipolar tendencies. They act one way and then suddenly do a complete turnaround, as if they have two different personalities; they can be nice one minute and explode the next.

10. Pushes for more intense involvement. Beware of the person who claims it was love at first sight and then presses for more physical involvement and a total commitment before you've really had a chance to get acquainted.

11. Shows destructive tendencies. If the person you're dating breaks or strikes objects, including cherished possessions, or throws objects at you, near you, or around the room, get out before you get hurt.

12. Uses force. It's abusive for people to get their own way by using force, pushing or shoving you, or physically restraining you if you try to leave the room. Leave before they threaten you with bodily harm with an object or weapon. Don't wait until they make good on their threat.

If you find yourself in an abusive dating relationship, don't downgrade yourself, thinking you deserve this behavior. Don't believe the lie that this is your only chance to have someone, and it's better to be abused than be alone. No one deserves abuse. You are valuable to God and He has good plans for your life. (You can read more about this in chapter 5.)

After learning about the dangers of dating, one can more easily understand why your parents were so cautious when you first started dating, or why they may sometimes express their concerns to you now. To a young, innocent person, these types of abusive, hurtful behaviors seem farfetched, and you might think *It could never happen to me.* But it could. That's why it's so important to go slowly and cautiously when you begin your search for that special person, and make sure you end up dating the right mate!

SOMETHING TO THINK ABOUT . . .

- Do you agree or disagree with the statement, "Being in love is not reason enough to marry." What are the dangers in believing "Love conquers all"?
- If you are attracted to someone who is double bonded, acts as a counselor or counselee, is overly dependent on you or parents, has unresolved problems of the past, or characteristics that you'd like to change, what should you do?
- How do you feel about dating a widow or widower?
- How do you feel about dating a divorcé or divorcée?
- How do you feel about dating someone with children?
- Have you ever found yourself in a dangerous dating situation? Looking back, what do you feel you should have done to avoid this situation?

CHAPTER 3:
WHAT ARE YOUR CHANCES OF BEATING THE ODDS?

Research shows that you will have the best chance of staying married—and being happily married—if you marry someone who is similar to you in age, race, cultural values, education, spirituality, and interests. It's true that opposites attract, especially where personality is concerned. But when it comes to stability in marriage, it's the similarities that bind individuals together, not the differences.

Headstrong love makes a couple think they can beat the odds and find happiness and lifelong fulfillment in marriage, regardless of what the research says. But before committing your life to another, prayerfully consider your age, racial, cultural, spiritual, and educational compatibility. Have you known each other long enough to really know each other? And do you have your parents' support? All these are important factors that will contribute to your marital success.

THE IMPORTANCE OF AGE

What does age have to do with marital satisfaction? Actually, maturity is far more important to a stable marriage than age, per se. You see, I've met some very immature forty-year-olds!

Young love can work, if you marry the right person. When my brother came back from his twenty-fifth high school reunion, he said that amid all the troubled and broken families, Liz and Greg still behaved like newlyweds. They had married when she was fifteen and he, just barely seventeen. Considering the odds, they shouldn't have made it. But they did.

Generally speaking, however, the older you are, the more you have experienced and the wiser you become; the more you have discovered who you are and what you like or dislike and what makes you feel good or bad. Therefore, the better your chances will be of choosing a mate most suited for long-term love and commitment. The high-school and college years are characterized by rapid change. When couples marry during this time, often their values and interests change, but they aren't willing to adapt and accept the changes in each other. In addition, younger couples usually don't have the resources to overcome crises that older couples have (e.g., a good savings account or a support system of mature friends).

Age differences can also affect a marriage. If there is too great a difference in age, not only will there be differences in interests, recreation, musical taste, and friends, but there is also the tendency of one to treat the other like a younger, less responsible person. Some men marry older women because they enjoy being mothered. Many women marry older men because they are unconsciously looking for a father-figure. Mothering and fathering, however, were not meant to be a part of the husband/wife relationship. Parenting may meet a psychological need at first, but it quickly grows old, and resentment sets in. It's also true that major age differences may not be that apparent at first. One might be just past teenage years and the other in the prime of life, but they can both enjoy similar activities. What happens, however, when old age creeps up and steals the energy or health of one while the other is still raring to go? It's not always easy for a couple to survive those differences.

Age differences become less important to older and more mature individuals—as long as the difference is not that great. It's not unusual for men and women in midlife to marry a companion that is five to ten years younger or older. In fact, an increasing number of women are marrying younger men. (There may be an advantage to this since men often die at an earlier age than women.) Making this choice when you're in high school or college, though, may result in conflict because men generally are not as mature as women during this period.

Remember, it's not the number of birthdays you have had that is important for marital success. It's how mature you are and whether you have enough similar interests and goals to carry you through the different stages of life.

RACIAL DIFFERENCES

Racial similarity is more important for the ease of marital harmony than young people tend to believe. It's common for racially mixed marriages to occur after the couple has been on a high-school or college campus where there is a blend of all types of races and cultures and there is a great deal of acceptance of cross-racial dating. The problem is that friends and family looking from the outside are not usually as generous. It shouldn't be this way, but the fact remains that it is.

After marriage, a racially mixed couple may find that it is more difficult to establish new friendships, especially if they live in a place where mixed marriages are frowned upon. Because of prejudice, they may need to move away from their families to a location where racially mixed couples are more accepted.

If one or both families openly disapproves, this can cause adjustment problems for the couple. Whenever there is a weakening of a couple's support system, there is additional stress placed on the marriage relationship. In addition, the couple must consider the children they may have. Because they will be a blend of two races, Will they be accepted by both? What special issues will they have to cope with by having racially mixed parents?

When cultural differences are added to racially mixed marriages, there is even more risk.

CULTURAL VALUES

Cultural differences can be like a pesky fly in an otherwise happy union. A person's upbringing determines his or her feelings about values, the way holidays are celebrated, how a woman is treated in the home, how money is handled, the type of language used, what expectations are held for the children, how they should be disciplined, food preferences, and on and on.

If you are serious about someone, don't plan a wedding until you have met your future mate's parents. Stay in each other's homes for two or more weeks—you will observe differences you never realized were there. (It's difficult for a family to put on an act for more than a week.) Not until then can you begin asking, "Will I be able to accept these differences? Do we have enough in common that we can adjust to the uncommon?" Are we willing to discuss ways we can make our cultural differences work for us and not against us? Are we willing to compromise for the good of each other?

Jessica grew up in a warm, accepting, informal Southern family who knew no strangers and had a hug of everyone. Her dad was gentle, kind, and soft-spoken. He had a special love relationship with each child. They could tell him anything, and he was never too busy to listen.

Steve had a northern European breeding. His dad was the undisputed head of the family. His word was law. His mom was an excellent cook and homemaker and was always the one the kids would go to when they needed comforting, while his dad rarely took time to read to the children or play with them. Steve never remembered his dad showing affection to his mom, even though he knew they loved each other. Their lifestyle was just more formal, social events were careful planned, and their physical demonstrations of love were few.

When Jessica spent Thanksgiving vacation at Steve's home, she had a rude awakening. Suddenly she and Steve had a whole new agenda of topics they needed to discuss about the differences between their two families.

It wasn't until Steve visited Jessica's home over Christmas vacation that he really understood what she was talking about. Jessica's family always had a house full of guests, and everyone received a warm, affectionate greeting. Hugging and public demonstrations of affections were hard for Steve. He never remembered his father spontaneously hugging anyone, not even the kids.

Would Steve feel comfortable being the affectionate father Jessica wanted for her children? Would he be the kind of husband who would kiss Jessica or say loving things to her in front of them? And what about spending time with the children? Jessica's idea of parenting was that it should be a shared responsibility. She didn't mind Steve being the head of their family, as long as he discussed everything with her first and they came to joint decisions, as her parents did. She knew she couldn't live happily with someone who considered his word law, regardless of how others felt. Another thing she noticed about Steve's family was that they talked only about business and material things, while her family talked about ideas and concepts, their dreams, and their feelings. Sharing feelings was especially important to Jessica.

Steve, on the other hand, valued more conventional roles. He didn't know whether he could accept the idea of Jessica working outside the home while the children were small.

As it turned out, they got married. Steve liked what he saw in Jessica's home. It was a refreshing change and an eye-opener to him. And if you would talk to Jessica today, she would tell you that Steve is a lot more like her dad than his own. But take note: not all individuals are able to adjust to another cultural background as easily as Steve did.

The way you are reared, the role models of Mom and Dad, and your cultural heritage will affect your expectations for your marriage. This doesn't imply that these differences make a person less or better than someone else—just different. How much better it is to discover these differences before marriage than to resent them later.

SPIRITUALITY

Similarities in spiritual interests and beliefs become extremely important after marriage. A critical stage is reached when the kids come along and a decision must be made about their spiritual instruction. Knowing and agreeing on where you and your boyfriend or girlfriend stand spiritually is vital to future marital happiness.

Just belonging to the same denomination is not enough. There can still be major differences in standards and convictions. In fact, there can be greater differences between two young people from the same church than there might be between two dedicated Christians who belong to different denominations.

Your spiritual belief system encompasses every aspect of your life, including such things as recreation, entertainment, and music. Some denominations have such a strong heritage of traditions and values concerning such things as Sabbath observance and lifestyle choices that it becomes vitally important not to marry outside your denomination.

During your courtship, look carefully at your belief systems. Talk about what's really important to each of you. How open are you to embrace the beliefs of the other? It will help to determine whether those beliefs are Bible-based or merely tradition. Learn more about each other's spiritual background by attending church and studying the Bible together. This can be an exciting growing time for both of you.

Discuss the spiritual leadership you want for your home and what role the church will play in your life. Realize however, that this may change once children are born. Before marriage, such things as attending church and embracing Bible doctrines may not be that important; after you have children, that will likely change.

Talk about your concept of God, the nature of Christ, the importance of God's grace and obedience to the law—including the Ten Commandments. Do you plan to keep one day of the week holy? Is it important to you that God said keep the seventh-day holy, meaning from sundown Friday to sundown Saturday? Are certain activities considered unacceptable Sabbath activities? What about giving tithe and offerings? What is your idea about speaking in tongues, the judgment, the state of the dead, perfection? Do you believe in a literal coming of Jesus? How does this affect the choices you make now? These are important doctrinal issues that should be discussed before marriage so you're not surprised afterward.

Sue married an inactive Jehovah's Witness. Since he didn't attend church, she never considered the importance of finding out about his belief system before she married him. It was a rude awakening for her when their daughter had surgery and her husband refused to approve the blood transfusion she needed.

Even though he wasn't a practicing Witness, this was still a part of his belief system.

Sarah grew up as a vegetarian in a Seventh-day Adventist family. She no longer practiced that lifestyle when she met and married Jamie. But when their children were born, Sarah decided to go back to the values she had been taught as a child. Jamie was surprised, but didn't resist. Instead, he adjusted to a meatless diet and enjoyed attending church with them on Sabbath. His openness to grow with Sarah enhanced both of their lives. Not every spouse is open to embrace lifestyle changes in the other. Instead of seeing change as beneficial, some resent it and make life difficult.

Most people who don't have a strong religious background or spiritual belief system marry thinking spiritual similarities don't matter. Once children come along, however, things often change. This seems to be especially true with women—but it can happen to men as well. Like Sarah in the illustration above, they want their children raised in a church. Even though it's impossible to know exactly how the person you're dating would react to a spiritual/lifestyle change in you, it's worthwhile discussing this possibility before marriage.

EDUCATION

The statistics seem to indicate that the more education you have, the better chance of a successful marriage. It's not, however, the number of years in school or the academic degrees that make marriages stable. It's that the more education people obtain, the more they learn about themselves and the better idea they have about the type of person they want as a life partners. And, ideally, the more education people receive, the wiser they become.

Discuss your educational goals. If one partner wants to pursue a graduate degree or professional training, that person will be changing significantly during this period. Is the other willing to grow too? Once one is finished with his or her education, will the other have a chance to go back and get more training, or be able to take some time to pursue their own interests?

Many marriages dissolve after one partner puts the other through school or professional training. Instead of appreciating the sacrifice of the one paying the bills, too often the more educated partner grows dissatisfied with the spouse. There is a greater disparity in their interests. Sometimes values change. When it's the wife who chooses to continue her education, a husband may resent the elevated status of her new career or the fact that she now earns more money than he does. Other men are happy for the increased earning power of their wives, but find themselves less motivated to pursue advancement in their own careers. This can cause their wives frustration and resentment. Women respect men who can and will financially support their families, regardless of whether or not their wives work.

Here's an interesting fact: Men tend to marry women who have educational goals similar to their mothers. If their mothers got a graduate degree, they are attracted to women with graduate degrees. If their mothers worked, they prefer women who themselves want to work after marriage. Find out how the person you're dating feels about this.

Growing together is the key to marital happiness. This doesn't mean if one chooses to get a degree that both should. But both should be willing to continue reading, learning, and moving forward on a self-improvement course. Find something that's meaningful to you, pursue it, and you'll find it rewarding. Be interested in the work and activities of each other so you can find fulfillment in discussing issues together. In addition to this, it is important that you help each other move forward toward God's potential for both of your lives.

My husband was the one who encouraged me to get my doctorate. He already had his. I had always loved books and learning, but I never thought I could get an advanced degree. I'm sure we would have lived happily with only one doctorate in the family, but having gone through the academic experience that he had gone through, we now have much more in common.

LENGTH OF COURTSHIP

Research indicates that long courtships (not engagements) are conducive to long marriages. Knowing each other over a long period of time (two years or more) allows you to see each other in many different situations. It reduces the surprise factor once you're married. As long as you've had a good friendship and serious dating has allowed you to get to know each other well, engagements shouldn't be longer than it's necessary to plan a wedding,

The longer you know each other—or the more intensely you are involved in each other's lives—the more chances you will have to observe each other in a wide variety of situations. A longer courtship gives you time to discuss your differences and be willing either to compromise or establish more cohesive habit patterns.

Here are some examples of what you can learn during a longer courtship:

How does he react when the car breaks down or someone curses at him or he loses his job? How does she handle the stress of a new job? Does she like to entertain? How are his manners? What's more important to him, Monday night football or a walk in the moonlight with you? How does he treat authority figures? How orderly does she keep her living space?

What really gets her down, and how long does it take before she snaps back? Is PMS (premenstrual syndrome) a problem? Does he have frequent headaches or bouts of depression? Do you respect his eating habits? Does it bother you that she doesn't take care of her body by eating a healthful diet and exercising?

Is he a show-off in front of his friends? Are you embarrassed by what she says? Will he accept church responsibilities? Does he choose to go hunting and fishing rather than spend extra time with you? Does she use her God-given talents? Does she like to cook? Does he offer to wash the dishes?

How does he keep his room, his clothing, his car, and his personal self? How does he feel about government and taxes? What are her political leanings? Does the music he listens to bother you? If she has a free evening, how will she choose to spend it? How does she feel about celebrating Christmas? What does he choose to do on vacation? How does he feel about spending or saving money? Will she buy on credit? And the list could go on and on.

In addition to all the things you're going to find out the longer you know the person you're dating, the more time you will have to talk about important issues that will impact your marriage. You'll find hundreds of questions to ask each other in the appendix to this book.

Remember, you can change after marriage—but because there may be less motivation to do so, it's always better if important changes can occur before the wedding!

PARENTAL ACCEPTANCE

Parental approval is another contribution to a lasting marriage. Your parents know you better than most other people do. If they have reservations about your choice, those reservations should be prayerfully considered. Talk earnestly with your parents. Listen respectfully to their concerns without becoming defensive. Fast and pray to determine the truth of their observations. And don't rush the relationship. Most parents object when they feel that you're just infatuated with each other and are blindly rushing into marriage without considering the problem areas that friends and family have noticed. If this is true, time has a way of working things out. Either your parents' insights will become apparent to you, or they will realize that their concerns were groundless.

Parents aren't always correct in their assessment of a potential mate for their adult child. They can have unrealistic expectations or object because they really don't know the person. Or they may have preconceived ideas about who you should marry and this person doesn't fit. Sometimes a Christian couple must deal with the irrational opinions of their non-Christian parents. So if time doesn't change your parents' opinions, seek the advice of a pastor or a trusted and wise professional who knows both of you well. Go through premarital counseling before you become engaged and consider carefully the results of your personality profiles. If the person counseling you points out major areas of concern, take what he says seriously.

At one of my seminars, Shelley's mom told me this story. Shelley and her parents were extremely close during her growing-up years, and the parents carefully monitored the boyfriends who showed up on their doorstep.

But college away from home brought added freedom, and Shelley began to date some questionable characters—at least her parents thought so. At first Shelley freely confided in her parents: "Hey, I've just met this really great guy named Michael. He's smart—a Merit Scholar—and comes from a wealthy family in Florida. Ah, he has kind of like, purple hair. He's really a nice guy, though, and so athletic. When you see him, I hope you don't mind the ring in his ear."

Their reaction was so negative that Shelley choose to not tell her parents any more about who she was dating. She ended up with a guy who didn't have purple hair and an earring, but he did have a rebellious and dominating spirit. He became possessive of Shelley. He resented her even phoning her parents because every time she did, their concern and counsel left her confused. Word leaked through to her mom and dad that this guy was on drugs and not en-rolled in classes, even though he masqueraded as a student.

After a home visit, Shelley went back to college determined to break up, but her boyfriend wouldn't listen. Instead, he talked Shelley into living in his moth-er's house, where she could be "protected" from her parents' interference. His mom wouldn't even let Shelley's parents talk to her on the phone.

Six months later, Shelley woke up to the fact that she was being manipulated by this possessive guy and his family. She moved out and thanked her parents for their continuing prayers. Shelley's parents were more than a little relieved she didn't marry this man.

The old cliché is true: when you marry, you marry the family. Why start out marriage with bitter feelings against parents and in-laws? With a little more time, relational differences are likely to resolve themselves. According to the Scriptures, true love never fails (1 Corinthians 13:8). If your love is true, it will pass the test of time until parents accept your union.

Studies verify the importance of age, race, parental approval, cultural values, education and spiritual interests when it comes to having a marriage that lasts. "But," say young lovers, "we're not statistics. We're not like everyone else. We'll never get a divorce."

There are exceptions to every rule, that's true. However, your chances for a happy, lifelong marriage are greater if these factors are considered carefully. When you note big differences, acknowledge them. Instead of immediately thinking this relationship is hopeless, consider if there is some benefit in stretching yourself to embrace these differences. Give yourself time before you commit to marriage to see if this relationship that is going to bring you the fullness of life that God wants for you. Remember, we're all created different. And not all differences lead to dysfunction. Some can lead to an exciting, adventurous, mind-expanding, joyful life journey!

Trying to beat the odds, however, is risky business in a world where Satan would like nothing better than to break up a home, destroying husband, wife, and children in the process. Proverbs 3:4–6 is good counsel to those who are serious about love: If you want favor with both God and man, and a reputation for good judgment and common sense, then trust the Lord completely; don't ever trust yourself. In everything you do, put God first, and he will direct you and crown your efforts with success (TLB).

SOMETHING TO THINK ABOUT . . .

- Have you and the person you're dating discussed your differences in the areas mentioned in this chapter?
- Do you see any points of potential conflict?
- In what ways are you alike?
- Plan now to set aside time this month to talk about these issues.

CHAPTER 4:
QUALITIES OF A GREAT DATE

You've probably thought a lot about your future mate. You may have described him or her in vague generalities, or perhaps you've gotten specific about the type of person you'd like to marry. I believe everybody should make a list of essential characteristics they want in a mate. Before reading this chapter, why don't you take a minute to make your own list? Compare your list to the traits I'll be talking about, adding any characteristics you feel you may have missed.

THE TRAITS I WANT IN A MATE

1. _____
2. _____
3. _____
4. _____
5. _____
6. _____
7. _____
8. _____
9. _____
10. _____
11. _____
12. _____
13. _____
14. _____
15. _____
16. _____
17. _____
18. _____
19. _____
20. _____

Take a good look at your list, and then remind yourself you'll never find a perfect mate because there is no such thing! We're human beings, after all. You need to decide which of the things you have listed are absolutely essential and which could be considered frosting on the cake. You can do this by either ranking your list, putting the most important traits at the top or by breaking your list into two categories: those traits that are absolutely essential, and those that would be nice but not absolutely necessary.

Traits Ranked in Order of Importance	Essential Traits
1._____	1._____
2._____	2._____
3._____	3._____
4._____	4._____
5._____	5._____
6._____	6._____
7._____	7._____
8._____	8._____
9._____	9._____
10._____	10._____

Finished? Let's move ahead.

The following are some traits I think are important for a good marriage partner to have. How do you feel?

TRAIT 1: A HAPPY DISPOSITION

Look for a happy, optimistic person. Find someone who has a sense of humor and can laugh at himself. It's not much fun to live with a negative, critical, pessimistic, complaining person or someone who habitually puts you, self, or others down. True happiness springs from a content heart. Beware of the person who is happy only when you are around. You're going to get tired of being responsible for another person's happiness. You could end up feeling guilty when that person slips into bouts of depression. It's easy to blame yourself and say, "If I were only a better person, she would be happy." And it's even easier to get tired and frustrated with having to live with someone's negative attitude.

Beware of the date who says, "I will be happy if you marry me, shave off your beard, lose five pounds, and get a new car." True happiness is not dependent on things. It's a part of a person's character, regardless of the circumstances.

If you think you're going to change a pessimist into an optimist, forget it. Lifetime habits of negative thinking won't change overnight. These negative traits can be repressed during the romance of a courtship, so the only way you will know if a real change has occurred is not to rush to the altar. Marry a happy person. Don't marry one that merely promises happiness.

TRAIT 2: THOUGHTFULNESS

Thoughtfulness is the trait that first made me sit up and take note of Jan—the man I would someday marry. Jan's sister, Chris, had an old clunker of a car. I'll never forget the night we took Jan back to the airport after our blind first date. He was in his business suit, white starched shirt, and tie. As he got out of the car, he said to his sister, "Chris, let me check your oil." I couldn't believe it! I had never heard of a guy being that thoughtful of his sister. Suddenly, I was interested.

How does your date treat his parents and yours? Chances are you'll get treated very much the same way. Does she see things that need to be done and offer to help? Or does he put his own needs first? Does he open the car door and wait to seat you at the table? Manners are important—and they seldom improve after marriage.

Thoughtfulness is other-centered behavior. It's the opposite of selfishness. A selfish person constantly looks out for his or her own well-being and has little or no concern for the interest and welfare of others. When you're dating, look for someone who puts others first, who is willing to go out of his way to help those who need it, or who sees how she could make a difference in someone's life by offering a helping hand or an encouraging word. Don't continue to date someone who puts people down in order to make himself look better. Don't marry someone who constantly talks about herself, what she likes, and how great she is. There's no room in marriage for selfishness. Great marriage partners put each other's needs first, and this type of other-centered thoughtfulness should first be demonstrated in the dating relationship.

TRAIT 3: NOT EASILY ANGERED

George was a talented, handsome guy, but he couldn't seem to control his anger. Little things set him off. For a while Missy put up with his mini–temper tantrums, like blasting the horn when a car cut in too close or yelling at his mother, "Don't tell me what to do!"

Missy tried to make excuses for his behavior, thinking he was tired since he had a full-time job and was going to business school on the side. When she finally brought up the subject of his temper, he got angry.

One night when George took Missy out to dinner, he discovered he didn't have any cash in his wallet. He had ID, but the restaurant wouldn't accept a check—and policy was policy. George argued, pounded his fist on the table, and finally yelled, "Get me the manager." Missy was embarrassed, left the restaurant, and broke the engagement.

Missy's decision was a wise one. Temper outbursts like this can be the symptom of internal hostility. This hostility is often repressed during courtship as a person is trying hard to be on his best behavior, but it will become more frequent and violent after marriage. Take seriously any outburst you observe, and check with others who have known this person in different situations to see if they have noticed this trait.

Do not marry a man with a history of hitting his mother, sister, or another woman in a temper outburst. If it happened once, it can happen again, and after marriage you or your children are likely to be the victims. Anger can also cause a wife to be abusive to her husband or family. The way a woman treats her younger brother may be an indication of how she will treat her husband.

Anger can be expressed in many ways, and the angry outbursts or temper tantrums that George threw are simply the most easily recognizable. Be equally leery of the person who has not learned to express anger in words and instead merely harbors angry feelings in his heart. Going silent and withdrawing from a loved one because of anger is unhealthy and damaging to a relationship. It's rejection par excellence.

Everyone experiences feelings of anger. The secret is to recognize the first signs and be willing to deal with the anger in a constructive way by talking it out, playing a good game of tennis, or cleaning the oven. Don't allow angry feelings to build, causing an uncontrolled explosion or a hostile silence.

Discovering the root of internal hostility and learning to solve problems without anger usually take professional counseling. The motivation for a guy like George to seek the help he needs to overcome his destructive behavior will be much greater before marriage than after.

Be sure you date a person long enough to observe how easily he or she becomes angry and how these angry feelings are expressed. Ask yourself, "Is this what I want to live with for a lifetime?"

TRAIT 4: WILLING TO SOLVE PROBLEMS

If you went by looks, Kent was probably the most desirable guy on campus, robust with gorgeous blue eyes and wavy dark hair. But his behavior was not nearly as attractive as his appearance. You see, Kent was never wrong—at least according to his own opinion. If mistakes were made, it was always the other guy's fault. He never said, "I'm sorry," because he wasn't. He was always right. Why solve problems? That would mean admitting that something was wrong. And compromise was out of the question.

When Kent started dating Julie, he thought he had found the perfect woman. She was gentle and hated conflict, so when they had a difference of opinion, she backed down. Sometimes she tried to reason with him and suggested a compromise, but her words fell on deaf ears. It didn't take her long to discover that they got along much better when she just accepted what he said and didn't argue.

They would have never gotten married had Julie realized that Kent wasn't going to change, or had Kent realized that Julie was. As Julie's self-confidence increased, she began to stand up to Kent. She learned that she could get her own way and avoid a conflict by merely doing things behind Kent's back.

And the result? A miserable marriage. When things hit a low, Julie threatened to leave until they got counseling. "Counseling?" exclaimed Kent. "Who needs counseling? There's nothing wrong with me!"

It's almost impossible to solve relationship problems by yourself. Marry someone who will be honest enough to admit being wrong, who doesn't have a habit of blaming others, and who is interested in solving problems. Marry someone who believes that God's way means submission to one another (Ephesians 5:21) and not just the wife to her husband.

Trait 5: Purity

Purity is not just an old-fashioned virtue. It's becoming more and more in vogue since the threat of AIDS and since the addictive power of Internet pornography. It's just safer to date someone who hasn't played around or someone who doesn't have a sexual addiction.

Plan now the circumstances under which you want to first have sex. If it's on your wedding night with you marriage partner, giving each other your gift of virginity, you should seriously consider the wisdom of dating someone who has already chosen to give his or her gift away.

At the same time you should not hold it against a person for past sexual involvement. Rebellion, ignorance, or being taken advantage of can rob a person of his or her virginity. Statistics tell us that even among Christian young adults, many have been involved in premarital sex. The important questions to ask are: What is my date's current commitment to purity? What were the circumstances of that previous sexual encounter? Was the sexual experience a revelation of true character that is being masked at this moment, or was it a mistake the person feels deeply sorry for and has vowed not to repeat? Choosing from this moment on to keep yourself for your marriage partner will make your wedding night special.

You cannot always judge a person's true purity by virginity alone. It has been estimated that at least one-fourth of all women have suffered sexual abuse and one-sixth of all men. We accept the fact that rape is all too common among young women, but we don't often consider that young boys and men are also sexually violated against their wishes.

If this has happened to you, you are not at fault. You did not choose this. You may have been the victim of a sexual experience, but this does not have to destroy your purity. However, this abuse can affect your future relationships unless you seek professional help.

If you are dating someone who has been sexually violated, don't get married unless that person has received counseling and expresses a willingness to get further counseling if remnants of the past begin to affect the marriage relationship. If you are engaged, the counselor may want to talk to both of you so you can gain insight into how this might affect your future. Often sexual problems in marriage can be triggered by past memories. Commit now to seeking counseling in the future should the need arise.

Mind purity is equally important. Is your date pure in his or her thoughts and speech, as well as behavior? What jokes does he tell? What music does she listen to? What movies does he watch? What books or magazines does she read? What Internet sites does he frequent? Are they pure or suggestive? Mind pollution can lead to disrespect of the opposite sex. You don't want to marry a crude, immoral individual. Nor do you want to marry someone who is addicted to pornography. The person you're dating may not frequent adult bookstores or topless bars, but may in the privacy of his or her own room be visiting sexually explicit Web sites that encourage masturbation and sexual experimentation. *Sexual addictions can destroy a marriage.* To date someone who has a sexual addiction, even though he or she may have other admirable traits, is playing with fire. Break up immediately, regardless of how much you're in love. Sometimes the threat of losing a loved one is the only thing that will shock a person into getting the professional help needed to break an impure habit.

TRAIT 6: TRUTHFULNESS

Too often couples play games when they are becoming acquainted. "I can't act as if I like him, because that would be too forward." "If I told him the truth, he might not like me." "I hate rock music, but I pretend it's OK because I don't want to hurt her feelings." Playing games in a relationship is a form of dishonesty. As long as games are being played, don't get serious.

Marriage isn't a game. It's a serious lifetime commitment. Your marriage will never pass the test of time if it is built on the sands of dishonesty. Search your own feelings and share honestly during your courtship. *Be you.* If what you say or what you do is misunderstood, how much better it is to find that out before you get married than have to suffer through a lifetime of misunderstanding.

Some people are habitual liars—a very serious character flaw. They lie without thinking and for no apparent reason. It will be impossible to build a stable marriage with a person who is basically untrustworthy.

But just how truthful should you and your date be about past behavior? What if you have had a drug or alcohol addiction or have served time? Should you mention you had been sexually active? Maybe you have been the victim of rape or abuse. Should the person you date be burdened with these facts? Each individual will have to determine when the specifics of his or her past behavior need to be revealed.

Casual dating does not require full disclosure. Only you can determine how much to tell. Usually details are not necessary. It may be enough to say honestly, "I'm not proud of everything I did in my past, but I would like to put that behind me and be judged for the person I have become. If our relationship continues to grow and we are considering a lifetime commitment to each other, then I think it would be important that we share anything in our pasts that might affect our future relationship."

Honesty, tempered with common sense, is the best policy. If you have a question about how much to tell, seek the advice of a counselor rather than your friends.

Trait 7: Good Health Habits

No one wants to marry a slob—and few do. The end result of poor health habits usually doesn't show up during the early twenties or thirties. By forty and fifty, though, such things as overeating, snacking between meals, little or no exercise, and smoking begin to take their toll. Too often people end up married to health problems that could have been prevented.

Seven health habits have been isolated as important for longevity. Look for someone who (1) sleeps approximately seven to eight hours out of twenty-four (too little or too much sleep may be a symptom of other problems), (2) eats breakfast, (3) doesn't eat between meals, (4) keeps a moderate weight—not too fat or too thin, (5) exercises, (6) doesn't smoke, and (7) doesn't drink.

As you hold hands with the campus beauty queen or stare into the eyes of the football hero, it is difficult to imagine being married to an unattractive, overweight, unconditioned person. But it can happen to you, unless you marry someone who practices good health habits.

Health habits are a very personal matter. What one may consider acceptable health habits may not fit the other. For one, a twenty minute walk a day is adequate. For another, nothing less than five miles of jogging will do. For one, it is enough to eat lean meat and only a sip of alcohol at social occasions. For another, good health means a vegetarian diet with no preservatives, sugar, or alcohol.

Because alcoholism can devastate a marriage, consider carefully a person's view of drinking. Social drinking can become problem drinking when stress triggers an increase in alcohol consumption. The safest policy is to look for someone who doesn't drink and has no desire to do so.

If you are engaged to someone who has grown up in an alcoholic home, it would be wise to attend together a series of Al-Anon classes (Alcoholics Anonymous for family members). Go to a counselor trained in substance abuse to discuss how this background may impact your future marriage. Alcoholism has significant and long-lasting effects on family members.

Drug abuse is equally harmful. Beware of the person who feels pills are the acceptable way to feel good, keep awake, go to sleep, or whatever else. Taking medication for every occasion can easily become a habit and lead to more addictive drugs that alter moods and behavior. It's best not to mess around with drugs, even those which can be purchased over the counter.

Health habits include body hygiene. Simple acts of brushing and flossing teeth or the frequency of bathing are important contributors to marital happiness.

Bad habits are difficult to break. That is why it's best to look for a person who has already established positive health practices or one who is committed to living a more healthful lifestyle, starting now.

TRAIT 8: ACCEPTS RESPONSIBILITY

Responsibility is usually a trait learned in the growing years, so if you see signs of irresponsibility, consider carefully whether or not you should continue the relationship. Otherwise you may find yourself in a similar situation as the following examples.

Kyle's mom kept an immaculate house—a place for everything and everything in its place. Growing up, Kyle rolled his eyes, but reluctantly put his stuff away when his mom got on his case. Since his friends complained about their moms too, he thought that's the way women were about their homes. It never dawned on him that Beth might be different—very different. When they were first married, he just figured that Beth, since she was working, was too tired to pick things up, so he picked up after her. But as the years rolled by, Kyle couldn't keep up with the clutter, and it became a major matter of contention between them. Why couldn't she notice when the clothes hamper was full? Couldn't she tell when food was rotting in the refrigerator? Taking responsibility was just not her cup of tea! Why hadn't he noticed this before marriage?

Tiffany and Jim have been married for eight years. For six of those years Jim hasn't had a job. At first Tiffany tried to blame Jim's erratic work history on his not finding the right position. But now, with two preschoolers and Jim once again jobless, Tiffany knows that's not the case. At least she expected Jim to take care of the home responsibilities while he was unemployed, but he didn't. Jim is just a happy-go-lucky person who doesn't like to be tied down to anything, especially not an eight-to-five job or the responsibilities of children. Tiffany is now so frustrated that she's sure she wouldn't have married Jim if she had realized just how irresponsible he was. But how could she have known?

Here are some questions that might detect irresponsibility:

Does he finish classes and projects he starts? Does she choose to complete homework and study for exams rather than party? Has he ever held a steady job? Does she see things that need to be done and do them? Does he volunteer to help? Does she get to places on time? Does he make lame excuses to get out of responsibilities? Does she take her talents seriously and work to improve her skills? Does he take care of his car and other personal possessions? Does she brag about getting out of work? Does he spend money wisely or impulsively? Does she pay bills on time? Does he keep his room clean?

Think about it. Just how responsible is the person you are dating?

TRAIT 9: GOOD SENSE OF SELF-WORTH

Clint talks about himself and how great he is. Lori puts herself down. Todd is constantly mentioning all the important people he knows. Jessie won't try anything new. Marta withdraws when she is in group situations. Tim frequently asks for affirmation, "How do you think I did?" Frank is a gossip. Leslie has a knack for slamming others and pouting. James often gets his feelings hurt.

What do all these people have in common? They are all suffering from low self-worth—and they suck the life out of you. People with low self-concepts don't make good marriage partners.

Often in a dating relationship, individuals with poor self-esteem gain a sense of value from the person they're with. They become dependent on their date to make them feel good. Sometimes they become like leeches, wanting the full attention of their date and resenting it and becoming jealous when he or she interacts with others.

Individuals with a negative self-concept sometimes have difficulty supporting and encouraging others. In some twisted way they think that if another person becomes successful, it will make them look worse. Some men suffer when their wives get a career promotion or make more money, for example. Some women cringe when their husbands are the life of the party. They resent the fact that the man they married has a great personality that just naturally attracts attention.

Tory was attracted to Heather because of her skill at the keyboard. They were both music majors, and they had a lot in common. Tory felt Heather was good for him because he had to practice hard to keep up with her. As their relationship developed, however, Tory grew resentful of Heather's natural talent and began competing with her for recognition and praise. Heather wondered why he never praised or encouraged her. He had been critical of her recital performance. At that point, red flags began to fly. Heather decided to discontinue the relationship, even though everybody thought they were perfect for each other because of their similar interests.

The next quarter Heather began dating a biology major. Rob knew very little about music, but he could sit for hours and listen to Heather play. He encouraged her and even made some contacts for her which resulted in a recording contract with an established studio. It wasn't long before Heather realized she was falling for this guy. This frightened her, since she had always pictures herself marrying someone musical.

When she talked to the dean of women about her dilemma, the wise woman said, "The secret to a successful marriage is to find someone who complements you, not competes with you. You should only marry when each of you feels so comfortable with your own talents that you can help the other become the very best he or she can be. You want a marriage partner who will help you reach your potential, not sabotage your efforts." That's good advice.

If you don't want to live a lifetime having to tiptoe around a person's fragile ego or having to hold yourself back for fear of how your spouse will react, then be careful not to get emotionally involved with someone who has a low sense of self-worth.

A person's self-concept can change. We all, at times, have suffered from feelings of inadequacy. Professional counseling is recommended if one is plagued with persistent feelings of inferiority or inflated superiority—both are caused by a low self-concept. A positive sense of worth is vital for marital happiness. Don't marry without it.

TRAIT 10: LIKES CHILDREN

You may think you'll never have children—but don't bet on it. If you do, you'll discover that a marriage will either be challenged or enhanced by kids.

Finding someone who likes children, understands them, and enjoys having them around is a real plus, if you want to have both a happy marriage and children.

Ted was a perfectionist. One time when he and Lisa were dating, a couple of little children came over to his car and touched it with their sticky fingers. Ted had a fit! He plowed those kids down with a stream of harsh adjectives as they fled from the scene. Later when they were visiting Lisa's older sister and her baby started to cry, Ted complained, "Why can't they keep that kid quiet?"

When Lisa asked him how he felt about children, he shrugged his shoulders and said, "They're OK when they stay in their place." That was enough for Lisa. She loved children and wanted to find a mate who felt the same way. Ted just didn't measure up.

Children should be a married couple's greatest blessing. Studies, however, show that couples with children are often less satisfied with their marriages than couples without children. The reason for this is twofold. First, it takes time to meet the needs of children. Parents sometimes neglect their needs as a couple because they are so busy with their children. Second, it's easy to disagree over how children should be raised. Before marriage you may discuss children, but unless you're around a lot of children and can observe your date interacting with them in a wide variety of situations, you really don't have any idea about how he or she may discipline your children in the future. Seldom do both parents totally agree on how a child should be raised. Finding someone who at least likes children is an advantage.

TRAITS 11: A PERSONAL RELATIONSHIP WITH GOD

It's very important for a marriage partner to have a personal relationship with God. Look for someone who is spiritually sensitive and willing to follow God's leading. A Spirit-filled life is one filled with love, joy, peace, patience, gentleness, goodness, faith, meekness, and temperance (Galatians 5:22, 23). A person who exhibits these traits is certainly easier to live with than someone who doesn't.

Beware of the person who gets spiritual just to win your affection or someone who says he loves the Lord, but doesn't act like it. You want to marry someone with a genuine Christian experience. Does your date talk about God? Can you discuss spiritual issues? Does he or she ever mention personal devotions? Do you ever see your date holding or reading a Bible? Do you enjoy going to religious meetings together? Does he have any speech or behavior patterns that seem inconsistent with a dedicated Christian? Can you pray together? Does being together help you grow spiritually?

Traci wasn't much interested in God when she first met Todd, and that's why she was nearly blown off her feet on their first date. After getting in his car to drive to a restaurant, Todd said, "I'd just like to ask the Lord to bless the time we spend together."

It didn't take Traci long to realize that Todd's faith was an integral part of him, not just something he put on for the weekend. And she liked it.

What about your date? If you're interested in a real Christian, make sure his faith is part of his life twenty-four hours a day.

TRAITS 12: ACCEPTS YOU JUST THE WAY YOU ARE

No one wants to go through life like a puppet on a string, constantly trying to win the approval of a marriage partner. Nor do you want to be the puppeteer pulling all the strings. If you go into marriage thinking you can change your mate, you'll be like the puppeteer, and your poor partner will be your puppet.

True love is unconditional love. This means that you are loved and accepted just the way you are, regardless of your size or shape, what you eat, how you keep the house, whether you have a high-paying job—or no job at all. Not until you love a person unconditionally, and you feel loved the same way, should you ever consider marriage.

Never marry a person just because you love his or her strengths. Loving good traits comes naturally. The important question to ask is, "Do you love what you consider to be her faults?" Only when you can truly love the total person, including all the weak points and bad habits, can you accept your mate for who he is and not secretly wish you could change him. Shy away from the person who thinks he or she can improve you, and without asking your permission puts you on an improvement plan. Watch the girl who is excessively straightening your tie or picking lint off your jacket. Be careful of the guy who tells you the right way to do something, or corrects your speech rather than listening to what you're trying to say. If this picky behavior is irritating before marriage, you can bet it will only get significantly worse afterward.

TRAIT 13: WILLING TO GROW

It has been said that growth is life; the opposite is death! So going into marriage, the concept of growth is very important for the fulfillment you want to experience. That's why you will want to marry someone who is willing and capable of growing at a similar rate as you. Ideally, this person is interested in reading self-improvement books, asking advice of experienced individuals, counseling with processionals if there is a need, attending marriage, birthing, or child-rearing classes, or joining growth groups. Marriage is never static. You can never know enough on your wedding day to get you smoothly through the various stages and crises of the family life cycle. Make sure the person you date seriously is the kind of person who is open to learning and will make changes when changes need to be made. Don't marry a selfish know-it-all!

Good marriage partners grow together toward full self-expression and the achievement of personal life goals. They encourage each other to maximize their knowledge, skills, and potential.

Be sure the person you seriously date agrees that the purpose of your relationship is to create an opportunity, not an obligation, for growth. Discuss together what makes your hearts sing, what you are enthusiastic about, what things light up your eyes, and what you get excited about. Whatever it might be: soap making, paddling, rock climbing, or learning more about natural healing, gourmet cooking, having a geothermal home, or organic gardening—whatever it is, are you willing to encourage each other in these pursuits and grow together?

TRAIT 14: AFFECTIONATE

I mention this characteristic last, not because it is the least important (it may be the most important), but because, before marriage, this trait can be tricky to assess correctly. During casual dating the expression of physical affection may get in the way of a couple getting to know each other as friends, while during serious dating, too much or too little affection may be misunderstood!

Regardless, appropriate affection is vitally important in a growing love relationship. This is especially true for women. Most women see affection as something that can be separated from sex. While men too often think of affection as the beginning stage for more intense petting and eventually sex.

Ann Landers conducted a survey on the importance of close, tender affection versus sex in the lives of women, and the findings were quite revealing. When asked if they would be content to be held close and treated tenderly and forget about "the act," the majority of women (72 percent) said Yes. Even women under forty voted for affection above sex.

Lucy's experience (I've changed her name to protect her identity) is just one example of how important affection is to a woman. Here is what she told me. "I was brought up in a strict home where my folks frowned on too much affection in a dating relationship. So when I became engaged, I just thought it was natural that my fiancé and I didn't express very much affection for each other. Once we were married, though, I expected things to be different. I needed expressions of affection, and was shocked and bitterly disappointed when my husband didn't change after marriage.

"He just was not an affectionate person. He never received affection as a child, so he didn't know how to give it. And he wouldn't allow me to be affectionate with him. Needless to say, I spent many lonely nights crying myself to sleep. Things got worse when the children came along. I don't ever remember him telling them that they were loved. And hugging and kissing were just not a part of his nature."

What happened to Lucy's marriage? Twenty years later, it fell apart. Affection is like glue in a marriage. Without it, it's almost impossible to hold a relationship together. When Lucy considered remarriage, she looked specifically for a warm, affectionate man.

How can you assess whether the person you are dating is an affectionate person when his or her lack of affection may merely be a wise choice to keep the relationship from advancing faster than your rationality? Or how can you make sure the affection that is shown to you is not just physical attraction being used as a powerful tool to entice you for sexual favors?

The answer is to look for tender words, acts, and touches that are given naturally and appropriately throughout the day and not just in private to initiate petting.

Appropriate affection is extremely important. One of my friends told me that his son brought a girlfriend home for Christmas who spent the whole vacation crawling all over him. It was sickening and highly inappropriate. The father worried how much longer his young son was going to be able to withstand such an onslaught of affection. If this was the way they acted in public, what must it be like in private?

This shallow affection is hot and passionate on a short-term basis only, and rarely continues after marriage—or after the person gets what he or she wants.

Another way to assess how the person you're dating feels about affection is to discuss how affection was shown in each of your families. Did you see your mom and dad touch each other? Was there much hugging and kissing among family members? Talk about your individual needs for affection that you both want in a marriage relationship. Can you live with what the other wants? As you advance toward marriage, you'll also want to talk frankly about the relationship between affection and sex.

One last thing. You may be wondering where looks or physical attractiveness ranks in a list of essential traits. I admit, looks are important, especially a neat and well-groomed appearance. Personally, I'd shy away from the guy with purple hair, tattoos, and an earring, and I'm not so sure most men would be attracted to a woman who is eighty pounds overweight. *But looks can change!*

What's really important is what's on the inside. Far too many young people use appearance as a sole criterion for judging a potential date. In doing so, they overlook individuals who would make great marriage partners. Why don't you do the uncommon thing and leave looks off your list? Concentrate on other essential traits. Chances are you'll be surprised how attractive a person becomes when you see the beauty of his or her character.

Each person will value the traits mentioned in this chapter differently, and there are many more that could be added to your list. Discuss with the person you're seriously dating what you consider essential characteristics in a marriage partner. It will give you some important insights into each other.

SOMETHING TO THINK ABOUT . . .

- Have you finished making your list of traits you want in a mate that was asked for at the beginning of this chapter? If so, how do the people you date fare when compared to your list?
  - What traits are optional?
  - What traits are non-negotiable?
  - In prayer, offer your list to the Lord, asking Him to work in the life of the person you will eventually marry, even though you may have not yet met that person.
- Read the following conversation between a man who asked a woman "What kind of man are you looking for?" Then discuss: How do you feel about the woman's answer?
  - Do you think this answer could be equally true if a woman asked a man the same question?
  - If not, how do you think the answer would differ?

In a brief conversation, a man asked a woman he was pursuing the question, "What kind of man are you looking for?"

She sat quietly for a moment before looking him in the eye and asking, "Do you really want to know?"

Reluctantly, he said, "Yes." She began to expound . . .

"As a woman in this day and age, I am in a position to ask a man what he can do for me that I can't do for myself. I pay my own bills. I take care of my household without the help of any man . . . or woman for that matter.

"I am in the position to ask, What can you bring to the table?" The man looked at her. Clearly he thought that she was referring to money. She quickly corrected his thought and stated, "I am not referring to money. I need something more."

"I need a man who is striving for perfection in every aspect of life." He sat back in his chair, folded his arms, and asked her to explain. She said, "I am looking for someone who is striving for perfection mentally because I need conversation and mental stimulation. I don't need a simple-minded man.

"I am looking for someone who is striving for perfection spiritually because I don't need to be unequally yoked. A believer mixed with an unbeliever is a recipe for disaster.

"I need a man who is striving for perfection financially because I don't need a financial burden.

"I am looking for someone who is sensitive enough to understand what I go through as a woman, but strong enough to keep me grounded.

"I am looking for someone who I can respect. In order to be submissive, I must respect him. I cannot be submissive to a man who isn't taking care of his business. I have no problem being submissive . . . he just has to be worthy.

"God made woman to be a helpmate for man. I can't help a man if he can't help himself."

When she finished her explanation, she looked at him. He sat there with a puzzled look on his face. He said, "You are asking a lot."

She replied, "I'm worth a lot." (From the Internet. Author unknown.)

CHAPTER 5:
HOW TO BE A GREAT MATE

Finding the right person will not necessarily insure marital happiness; being the right mate, however, may. So before going in search of your Mr. Right or Ms. Perfect, why don't you take a good look at yourself and ask, "Would I make a great mate?" First of all, how do you measure up on the fourteen traits mentioned in the last chapter?

1. Do you have a happy disposition?
2. Are you thoughtful?
3. Are you not easily angered?
4. Are you willing to solve problems?
5. Are your thoughts and behavior pure?
6. Are you truthful?
7. Do you practice good health habits?
8. Are you responsible?
9. Do you have a good sense of self-worth?
10. Do you like children?
11. Do you have a personal relationship with God?
12. Do you unconditionally accept others just the way they are without trying to change them?
13. Are you willing to grow to become a better person?
14. Do you show appropriate affection?

What does it take to be a great mate? All of the above, plus! That's a pretty tall order, isn't it? In fact, it's probably easier to find the right mate than to be the right mate. Being the right mate means the chances are good you're going to have to make some changes in your life.

Let's take a look at some of the qualities you'll need in order to be the right mate for someone special. Keep in mind that no one can be perfect in all these areas—just be willing to grow and change toward the ideal.

VALUING AND ACCEPTING YOURSELF

People who make great marriage partners don't have to be married to be happy. They are confident in who they are and don't mind being alone. They are complete in Jesus Christ and feel comfortable with themselves. They like who they are.

Wait a minute. Doesn't that sound too self-sufficient? Shouldn't marriage partners need each other? Well, yes—and no!

Yes, they should need each other but only because they enjoy meeting each other's needs. And no, they shouldn't be dependent on each other for their needs to be met.

Partners in a dependent relationship are skating through marriage on thin ice. What if something happens and one marriage partner can no longer meet the needs of the other? Is there enough unselfish love available that the marriage won't come unglued?

Look at it this way. Let's say you marry someone because that person makes you feel comfortable when you are in public, and you need that feeling of security. But what happens when that person has to go away on a trip and you must attend a social function alone? Will you resent your spouse leaving you at that time? Will you complain and make life miserable every time business takes him or her out of town?

If you need someone's presence in order to feel secure and comfortable, you are likely to try and control that person to keep him or her as close to you as possible. During the first few months after marriage, it might feel rewarding to meet the dependence needs of a mate. But it won't take long for this responsibility to become a burden from which the mate will want to escape.

How can you be sure that you don't marry another person because you need that person to feel fulfilled? Concentrate on valuing and accepting yourself. You can accept and value someone else only as much as you accept and value yourself. If you don't like who you are, the chances are great that you will try to find a partner who makes you feel better about yourself. You use that person to meet your unmet needs, and that's how unhealthy emotional dependence begins.

To avoid emotional dependence, concentrate on developing self-value and acceptance. Here's how to get started.

UNDERSTAND HOW VALUABLE YOU ARE TO GOD

God considers you a person of immeasurable worth. He's crazy about you. Take some time to read and study what the Bible has to say about you. You'll discover that you are valuable because:

- God created you (Psalm 139:13–16).
- God knew you and what you would become before your birth (Jeremiah 1:5).
- Jesus died to save you. In fact, He would have died just for you (John 3:16).
- God is preparing a home in heaven for you (John 14:1–3).
- God calls you His child (1 John 3:1).
- God rejoices over you as His bride (Isaiah 62:5).
- God needs you to represent His character to the universe (Job 1:6–8).
- Christ changes our lives by covering our "filthy-rag righteousness" with His robe of righteousness (Isaiah 64:6).

Look up the following verses and see how they make you feel. To make the experience even more meaningful, read these passages from a number of different versions. If there is a verse you find encouraging or that stands out, focus on that one first. You might even want to memorize it.

Psalm 8:3–6
Jeremiah 29:11
Jeremiah 31:3
Zephaniah 3:17
Matthew 17
Luke 15:8–10
Galatians 2:20
Philippians 3:20, 21
Philippians 4:13
1 John 3:2
1 John 3:24
1 John 5:19

Realize That Nobody's Perfect

If you doubt God's acceptance of you because you aren't perfect and don't feel worthy, check out the following texts:

- Psalm 18:30: "As for God, His way is perfect." (The verse doesn't say we have to be.)

- Matthew 19:21, 22: Jesus told the rich young ruler if he wanted to be perfect, he was to give away everything to the poor and follow Him. Jesus knew that this man had put his worldly possessions in front of his love for God. According to Christ, the way to "perfection" is to put God first, and follow Him. It doesn't mean never making another mistake.

- John 17:23: Without Jesus within us we can't be perfect.

- Colossians 1:28: Paul says the reason they preach Christ is so everyone can be presented perfect in Christ. (Outside of Christ, perfection doesn't exist.)

- Hebrews 7:19: The law (or doing right things) makes no one perfect.

- Hebrews 12:23: People are made perfect. (They don't get that way themselves.)

- James 3:2: We all make mistakes. If we didn't, James says, we'd be perfect. (His assumption seems to be that no one is perfect.)

The above texts may seem to contradict what Jesus said in Matthew 5:48: "Therefore you shall be perfect, just as your Father in heaven is perfect." However, read this passage in context. Jesus is delivering His sermon on the mount and has just given guidelines on how people should behave toward their enemies. He says if we can love our enemies (which is probably the hardest thing in the world to do), we'll be perfect because that's the way God is. It doesn't say that perfection is the ticket to God's acceptance. Just look at King David, who was called a man after God's own heart (1 Samuel 13:14), and you'll realize perfection isn't a requirement in God's kingdom. David seduced a woman, got her pregnant, had her husband killed, and then lied about it. Obviously it wasn't his behavior that made him a man after God's own heart. Rather, it was his attitude of repentance without casting blame, combined with his ultimate desire to have God create a new heart within him (Psalm 51:10) that drew him close to God.

TAKE AN HONEST LOOK AT YOURSELF

Embrace your story. All of us have a history. Good things happen—and so do the bad. Don't let the past pull you down and make you think less of yourself. Learn from your experiences because that's what makes you, *you*. Indeed, like the refining of gold in the fire, within your suffering, pain, and tragedy is hidden the treasure of who you really are. Shift your mind-set from "Woe is me," to "Wow, I have learned so many valuable things that can help me be a better person!"

With this thought in mind, write down all the traits you like and dislike about yourself.

Traits I like about myself	Traits I dislike about myself

Now compare your two lists. Which one is longer? You might show your list of traits you dislike about yourself to one or two trusted friends for their confirmation. If they don't see the negative traits you listed, you may have been too hard on yourself.

Now take your dislike list and think of one thing you could do to help you overcome each negative trait. If you are actively working on a self-improvement plan, you will feel better about yourself.

Here's how to begin your makeover: make a choice to change. Envision yourself as already changed and keep that vision alive by writing it down or posting a picture of someone or something that reminds you of your goal. Become aware of your negative behavior just before it happens or when it happens, and say to yourself, "This is *not* who I am," and stop immediately. Try to avoid circumstances that lead you to that behavior. In other words, avoid temptation! And when you are successful, believe yourself to be the new you from this moment on.

Warning: don't try to be perfect—and then when you fail, beat yourself up. Instead, claim God's promise in Philippians 4:13, "I can do all things through Christ who strengthens me." No one wants to live with a perfectionist! Remember, it's the process of working toward becoming a better person that counts, not the ability to never make a mistake.

Post your "like" list in a place where you will see it often, such as your bathroom mirror. Each time you see it, read it and say, "Thanks, Lord, for making me with these traits." God made you special. How must He feel when you don't value yourself? After all, you are His creation, and He doesn't make mistakes!

EVALUATE YOUR PROGRESS

Periodically, evaluate how well you are doing on developing self-value (through Christ) and self-acceptance. Are you less frustrated? Are you easier and more fun to be around? When you're making changes because you want to make them, and not because you think others expect you to change, it will bring you a sense of personal satisfaction. Here's an example.

For years Michelle felt frustrated and guilty when her house wasn't clean because she felt that was her responsibility, and she wanted to please others. One day it dawned on her, she liked a clean house. Now she does it for herself because she knows it makes her happy and the result is that she's much more successful.

Consider these two questions.

The first is, Do I value others? You can't value and accept others unless you value and accept yourself. Don't think about marriage until you can unselfishly serve others, putting their needs above your own. Marriage requires this type of self-sacrifice.

The second question is, Am I willing to grow? When you value and accept yourself, you will have the courage to begin making changes in your life. It's always easier to see how others should change than to muster the energy it takes to change yourself. But marriage requires change from you. You can no longer live a selfish existence. Because you knit your life together with another person, everything you do will affect your marriage partner, and everything he or she does will affect you. To blend your lives together into one is going to mean that you both must be willing to compromise. And you both must be willing to change.

Accept the fact that you aren't perfect: a willingness to change for the better makes you great mate material.

DEALING WITH THE PATHOLOGY OF YOUR PAST

Bob is a forty-six-year-old physician who has been married and divorced twice. He once commented to me that both of his marital failures could have been prevented if he had received the psychological help he needed before his first marriage. "Love is not enough to overcome personal pathology," he said.

After the break-up of his second marriage, he was devastated. In the depth of his despair he sought help. During the process of counseling, he was given a battery of personality tests, and when he looked at the results he was stunned. He went off the scale on the dominance factor. He knew he had an internal need to control, but he just thought it was normal.

In talking about his childhood to a counselor, he discovered the roots of this pathology. His parents were eastern Europeans who came to this country when he was six. Whatever his mother said, he did. If not, he knew his father would use a belt on him. He hated this and grew to resent his parents controlling his life. In fact, he resented anyone controlling his life. He developed an attitude that whatever his parents wanted him to do, he'd do the opposite. His younger brother was the same way. When the folks wanted his brother to become a physician, he took nuclear physics in college. His brother has never really been happy in his career choice, but he would never admit it to his parents.

When Bob first came to this country, he was teased by the other kids in school because he didn't know the language and behaved in a culturally different manner. He soon found, though, he could control his peers by cool, calculated, stand-off behavior that caused others to become uncomfortable and finally give in to him. Because of this, many of his acquaintances thought he was stuck-up. He tried not to let their criticism hurt by convincing himself they were wrong and he was right. He thus became highly opinionated and would not give up until he convinced others he was right. He also developed a need to always have the best. He thought he could flaunt high-fashion clothing, the best car, an expensive watch or tennis racket, and other people would notice and accept him.

The problem came when he carried this pathology into marriage. He chose a woman who was a very popular and talented campus leader. Throughout the courtship he was always fearful of losing her to someone more in her league, so he never left her side and spoke quite negatively about her friends in an attempt to separate her from them. After marriage, his need to control became even stronger. If she didn't do what he wanted, he tried to control her with his anger, or he withdrew his love. As her respect for him diminished, she grew stronger in her defiance and began exerting her own will. This brought tension and conflict. And the result? During one of his pouting times, she found someone who accepted her, and she had an affair.

The sad fact is that Bob's second marriage was almost an exact repeat of the first. How unfortunate it was that Bob and his first wife didn't have more intensive premarital counseling. Such counseling could have brought his pathology (and perhaps some of hers) to the surface so it could be dealt with and healed before it destroyed the marriage. But then, Bob and his fiancée were so in love and emotionally dependent on each other, they probably wouldn't have listened.

WHEN PERFECT ISN'T GOOD ENOUGH

Another area of pathology many people suffer from is perfectionism. A perfectionist is a person who isn't satisfied with excellence—he wants more. He attempts the impossible and then feels guilty when he can't attain it.

Tiffany struggled with these feelings all her life. She was a physically beautiful child, highly intellectual, and multitalented. Everyone expected miracles out of her because she could produce them. She began to feel she had to perform to perfection to be accepted. Her parents and friends didn't feel this way. They just knew that Tiffany, in doing her best, would do an outstanding job. But this is how she perceived they felt.

Tiffany's desire for acceptance resulted in pathological behavior. Knowing she wasn't perfect and feeling somewhat unworthy of unconditional acceptance, she began to seek acceptance by giving to others. In his classic book, *Four Loves,* C. S. Lewis calls this "gift love." Her behavior led Tiffany to choose boyfriends whom she could help. Her parents and friends couldn't understand Tiffany. There were many talented boys on campus, yet she chose to date and eventually marry someone who was not as social, intellectual, or spiritual as she. Tiffany had her reasons, though. The man she married needed her skills to fill in for his inadequacies. He became dependent on her to gain him social acceptance, to help him academically, to write to potential graduate schools, and to fill out job applications. And she didn't have to worry about feeling guilty if she wasn't perfect because it didn't matter to him. It was a comfortable relationship and highly satisfying emotionally.

He didn't perceive any need to have her help him spiritually, although this lack was what first drew her to him. He had a very shallow experience with the Lord, and Tiffany had just come back from a summer mission experience overseas and was bubbling over with enthusiasm. When her interest in helping him spiritually was not appreciated, she went overboard in the other areas, even causing her own grades and social activities to suffer. And because he didn't appreciate her spiritual fervor, that aspect of her life slowly diminished.

Because of the mutual dependence in this relationship, it felt satisfying to both. They needed each other—and they considered themselves the perfect match.

But shortly after marriage, the illusion began to fade. Tiffany realized her husband wasn't perfect. In fact, he had a long way to go. Immediately she put him on a self-improvement plan so he would become the perfect husband. He didn't take that for long. As he began to resent her help, she turned her attentions to others who were in need and appeared far more accepting of her abilities.

As a perfectionist, Tiffany never felt worthy of acceptance unless she was giving "gift love" to others. This giving, however, caused feelings of emotional dependence in relationships outside their marriage. Only Tiffany's strong moral code kept her from becoming physically involved. These relationships usually lasted as long as the other person would accept Tiffany's "gift love." Tiffany never saw any danger, but these relationships nearly destroyed her marriage.

The crisis came when one relationship lasted so long that emotional dependence turned into feelings of love. Both parties began to desire physical intimacy. Tiffany was living in an illusion that this was the perfect relationship. Only her moral standards wouldn't allow her to give herself sexually to someone other than her husband.

When she began to realize that this relationship was more important to her than her relationship with her husband or God, she became frightened and sought help. Through counseling, she and her husband were able to understand the pathological dynamics that were happening in their marriage and Tiffany began to work on overcoming her perfectionistic personality. They're still together, but it's been a rocky road.

If only Tiffany (and probably her husband) hadn't brought emotional hang-ups into their marriage. If only these hidden agendas could have been discovered before marriage, I wonder if they would have chosen to marry each other?

A wise mate faces the pathology of his or her past and deals with it before marriage, regardless of the time it takes or the cost involved.

MAKING MATURE DECISIONS

Decisions are personal choices based on values and needs. It is possible for two people to make completely opposite choices, and yet both would be making decisions that are good for them because of the differences in their values and needs.

Mature decisions are not impulsive decisions based on immediate gratification. Mature decisions are made when all the options and possible consequences have been carefully considered. To make mature decisions you have to be willing to gather the information you need to make informed choices.

Let's say you want to purchase a car. What do you need to know in order to make a good decision?

- Is this the best car for the money?
- Do you have enough money to purchase it?
- Do you really need a car right now?
- How much is the insurance?
- Is this the best time to purchase the car?
- What impact will this car have on your current life? (In other words, what will you have to give up in order to have enough money for its purchase?)

One engaged young man purchased a car that put him $8,000 in debt. In all honesty, he didn't need the car for another six months, and by then the next year's models would be available. Still, he purchased the car based on assumptions that turned out to be false. He assumed he would get a full-time, good-paying job right out of college. He didn't. In turn, he didn't have enough money for the insurance, so he stored the depreciating car in a garage. When he did get a job, he had to work weekends to keep up the car payments. He and his fiancée no longer had all the special time they used to enjoy together.

Before his car was even out of storage, another assumption proved false. He had assumed his fiancée would get a job during their first year of marriage so they could make car payments, and he could go to graduate school. Now, she was considering graduate school too. Would the purchase of this car rob him of getting an advanced degree and affect his career? He began to wonder if the car was worth it.

Mature decision makers aren't afraid to seek—and take—advice from those who are more experienced. Mature decision makers won't make a decision until all the information is in, and the consequences are carefully weighed. Mature decision makers aren't impulsive decision makers.

In the area of finances, mature decision making is critical. A few bad choices can put a newly married couple in debt for a lifetime, enslaving them to the lender and destroying their aspirations. For example, because of financial obligations a couple may have to work longer hours, leaving them without time or money for the vacations they had wanted to take. Their debt is like a wet blanket dampening their dreams.

To determine if you are making wise and mature decisions, ask yourself these questions:

1. *Am I willing to deny immediate gratification for long-term life goals?*

2. *Am I living a balanced life?* All work and no play isn't good for your health—and can destroy a marriage because there is little or no time for each other. Begin living a balanced life spiritually, socially, intellectually, and physically before marriage, and it's easier to maintain one afterward.

3. *Am I clear on my life goals? Do I know what I want to achieve? What is it going to take for my dreams to come true?* Finding yourself and getting the education you need will make you a much more desirable marriage partner. Without the burden of trying to combine school and a job, you will be able to concentrate on your spouse and your relationship even more.

4. *Have I established trustworthy friendships with people who have a positive*

influence on me? It isn't healthy to have all our emotional needs met in the person you marry. Friends enrich a marriage. Before marriage, cultivate friendships with others. They can provide social stimulation that is healthy for a marriage. If your friends make you feel inadequate or tempt you to participate in things you know you shouldn't, reevaluate. You don't need them. Remember this helpful motto: "Be a good friend and you will find a good friend."

DEVELOP YOUR SPIRITUAL LIFE

There is nothing as important as a personal relationship with the Lord to get you through the difficulties that all couples experience. When you and your spouse can pray together, share Bible promises, and seek the way you should go based on biblical principles and promises, you have a major advantage over couples who don't. Your chances of ultimately experiencing a lifelong marriage of happiness and fulfillment are significantly greater.

Here's one example of what I mean. A married couple had been separated for more than a year when they gave their hearts to the Lord and decided to try living together again. They agreed to no longer trust themselves for solutions to their problems. Instead, they went together to the Lord and had what they called a "white knuckle" prayer. They would grasp each other's hands, interlock their fingers and begin to pray. "Lord," Joe would say, "You know I can't stand it when Mary starts to nag. But, Lord, You can take anything. Help me respond as You would respond rather than impulsively reacting as I feel like doing. And Lord, if You could change Mary just a little, I'd sure appreciate it." And then Mary would pray a similar prayer: "Lord, I can't stand it when Joe tells me he is going to do something but doesn't. Give me Your patience. But if You could also help Joe to be a little more responsible, I'd be thankful."

How did prayer solve their problems? First of all, it allowed time for tempers to cool so Joe and Mary could think more clearly. Second, prayer helped Joe and Mary to be open to the Holy Spirit's influence. At that point, they were more willing to compromise or look for creative answers to formerly unsolvable conflicts.

Another way a relationship with the Lord can help a marriage is that instead of allowing your negative feelings to hurt your spouse, you can get them out by sharing them with the Lord. For example, wives sometimes irrationally feel neglected. Let's say your husband faithfully takes you out for a dinner date each week. One week he misses the date because of a business meeting which may ultimately mean advancement in his career. You shouldn't feel neglected, but you do. How should you respond? Give your feelings to the Lord. Say, "Lord, I'm feeling neglected, but I know it's not true. Help me overcome these feelings and replace them with something positive. Help me find the promise I need in Your Word that will make me feel good once again." In addition, ask God how you can grow during this time. Ask Him to give you wisdom, discernment, and creative ideas. Prayer works. It really does.

You will find that developing a close relationship with the Lord before marriage will be an incredible advantage afterward. A Spirit-filled life produces love, joy, peace, long-suffering, kindness, goodness, faithfulness, gentleness, and self-control. It's qualities like these that make a great mate.

GUIDE FOR GROWING GOOD RELATIONSHIPS

Before you can date the right mate, you have to meet the right mate. Maybe you're a novice at this thing called dating. Maybe you're not worried yet about a lopsided love relationship—because you're at ground zero. You want to meet interesting people. You want to be attractive to the opposite sex. You want close friends. You want people to like you and want to be around you. You want to have a wide variety of acquaintances from which to choose one or two to get better acquainted with. Maybe you're not really serious about love right now, just interested. You know what kind of relationships you want to avoid— all those that were mentioned previously in this chapter. But at the same time you don't want to drive people away or lose a potentially good girlfriend or boyfriend by weird or obnoxious behavior. Do you want to act smart? If so, here's your *Act Smart Dating Guide*!

BE FRIENDLY

Just like the proverb says, to have friends you must be friendly (Proverbs 18:24). If you're shy—and many are—you're going to have to practice being friendly. People who act shy are often accused of being aloof or conceited. You don't want that. So, here's the challenge: you've got to go where people are— especially to places where activities are going on that you're interested in. That means you've got to get out of your cave and get involved in activities you enjoy.

Here's an idea: force yourself to acknowledge every person who comes within ten feet of you. How? Smile, wave, say hello, look them in the eye, and if they stop close to you, say something! But what? The weather's always a safe topic. "Nice day!" "It looks like rain." "Wow, it's really windy."

Once you've made someone's acquaintance, a safe topic is an honest compliment. "That's a great color on you." "I like your boots." "Your hair looks great." Or you may choose to comment on something that you both have in common: "What did you think of the assembly speaker?" "Have you seen Joe lately?" "Did you hear the news about the airplane crash?"

Caution: don't be obnoxiously friendly. By breaking the ice with a smile, a hello, or a simple comment, you've done your part. If the person ignores you, is preoccupied with something else, or merely grunts, then let that contact go. Don't be so overly friendly that the person will try to avoid you in the future. If a friendship is meant to be, the person will respond positively.

You can get a lot of practice being friendly by looking for people who look as lost as you might feel. Usually these people are alone, have a sad expression on their face and slumped shoulders, and are staring at the floor. In other words, they look miserable. That's your chance. The person doesn't have to be date potential. It might be an elderly person or a kid; a janitor or a frustrated mom with preschoolers. Practice doing what Jesus would do. Lift them up with a smile; say something cheerful; ask if you can help; pray with them. You'll be surprised what a difference you can make in their lives, and in the process you'll get lots of practice that will help you be more friendly with your peers—and potential dates.

BE POSITIVE—SMILE INSIDE AND OUT

I can't express enough how important a positive attitude is. People like to be with people who are optimistic and cheerful. It's not that difficult to smile. And when you do, people will be drawn to you, and you'll feel better. A little song I sang as a child says it well: "Smile, smile, smile, and keep right on a-smiling. . . ."

Stop negative thinking. You might need to pray yourself out of those troublesome emotions that most young people suffer from. I have a handy resource for you that you won't want to leave home without. It's called *Passionate Prayer Promises.*[1] I wrote this book with Brenda Walsh to teach people how to pray by claiming Bible promises. I'm sure you'll find just the prayer and Bible verses you'll need to conquer doubt, fear, grief, guilt, jealousy, lust, pride, stress, or trials. There are one hundred ten topics from *A* (anger and anxiety) to *W* (work and worry). Pray yourself positive.

Every time you're tempted to talk negative talk, such as criticism or gossip, stop and say something positive instead. You can retrain yourself, and when you do you'll find people will enjoy being with you.

Laugh. Be fun to be with. Express the joy of the Lord, and let the sunshine of your soul light up the room. Let Psalm 118:24 be your theme song: "This is the day the LORD has made; / We will rejoice and be glad in it."

LOOK ATTRACTIVE

You don't have to shop in expensive stores and wear the latest fashions to make friends, but it sure doesn't help to look like a slob. Make sure you have a couple outfits that really look good on you. If you don't know what to buy, ask a friend who has the knack of picking out great outfits to go shopping with you. Don't dress to stand out. Dress to accentuate who you are. Dress to attract the type of person you'd like to marry someday. In other words, if you don't want to marry a playboy—or girl, don't dress to attract that type of person.

Dress isn't everything. You'll find you look better when you stand up straight, get rid of the flab, clear up skin problems, and keep your hair clean and stylish.

Why is appearance so important when God says it's what on the inside that counts? (1 Samuel 16:7.) Because men—and women—look on the outside! Attractiveness (along with being friendly and positive) is the first test given to new acquaintances. If you pass, then you have a far greater chance of at least beginning a relationship. The following seven guidelines will assist you in playing the dating game.

BE A GOOD CONVERSATIONALIST

Being a good communicator is such an important relational skill, I've devoted chapter 11 to the topic. I'll just give you three suggestions to get you started on the right track:

- Don't talk about yourself unless asked.
- Show a deep interest in the other person, asking questions and listening carefully—with plenty of eye contact.
- Don't talk too much—or too little. You'll get an A in Dating Com-

munication 101 if you allow the other person to do most of the talking. On the other hand, don't sit there like a bump on a log merely saying "Yes" or "No" because you're afraid of saying too much. Be engaging, fun, meaningful, and leave something to be said the next time you get together.

Women are attracted to men who are good communicators. Generally, that means they like men who are open and honest about their emotions and are not just information givers. On the other hand, men are intrigued by women who have something meaningful to say about such things as sports, politics, and the economy. But don't put on an act. Good communicators are honest and upright.

DO AND ACT YOUR BEST WHEREVER YOU ARE

You never know who's watching you. Few people are impressed with those who give only a mediocre performance when they could have given an Oscar-winning one. Everyone likes a winner. Few are interested in dating someone who is wasting his or her potential.

If you're in college, study hard, show you're interested in the subject, and ace those exams. At work? Give it your all. Put more into your job than you're paid to do. Be a contributor, not a taker. And consider carefully where you go. Do you really want people knowing you frequent the places you do? In short, clean up your act if you want to meet quality people.

At social gatherings, remember WWJD? (What would Jesus do?) That will help you put your best foot forward. You'll make some social errors. Everyone does. Just apologize, make amends if necessary, and learn from your mistakes. Never think that someone is so low on the social ladder that they don't deserve respect. You'll be judged by potential dates according to how you treat those in the service industries and blue-collar jobs, such as waiters, janitors, maids, bus drivers, and maintenance personnel. The kind of person you may want to marry may not feel safe with you if you treat others with disrespect.

GO PLACES WHERE YOU'LL MEET THE RIGHT KIND OF PEOPLE

Carefully consider what type of person you want to meet, and go where they might hang out. If you want someone who has the same religious belief, go to church functions and get involved. You might broaden your horizons by going on mission trips, attending regional or state convocations, and making friends with church families. You never know who has a younger sibling or friend that you might be introduced to.

Be careful about attending parties and certain entertainment events. If the wrong crowd is there and questionable activities are going on, you may get tagged with a negative reputation that you'll find hard to live down. Most people believe the maxim "Birds of a feather, flock together."

BE INTERESTING; DO INTERESTING THINGS; GO INTERESTING PLACES

Don't stay home or get bogged down in a boring weekly routine. Even if you enjoy doing certain things again and again, force yourself out of your comfort zone. If you're an interesting person, you'll find far more interesting people to date. Every new activity you participate in can be a springboard to finding new friends and potential dates.

DEVELOP YOUR TALENTS

Don't waste your time in a frantic search for your ideal mate. If you are using your time wisely, keeping your social life and your work or school life balanced, chances are quite good that the right mate will find you. This is especially true if you continue to develop and use your talents. Maybe it's music. Someone may notice you when you sing for church. Maybe it's sports. It's quite likely someone will hear about your skills and be interested. Whatever your talents, develop them. Few people want to waste their time with someone who is wasting his or her potential. Lazy people don't get very far in the dating game.

VOLUNTEER

There is no better way to meet new and interesting people than by volunteering to help people and projects. The world is full of volunteer opportunities. Take advantage of them. Chances are the person you would someday like to marry will be attracted to someone who unselfishly helps others, someone who sees a need and meets it.

BE YOURSELF

Be confident and secure about who you are. Men are not attracted to girls who kiss up to them, who make weak plays for affection, or complain to get what they want. And women aren't interested in wise guys who talk like they know it all, cool dudes who show off their sports car and brag about who they know, or romeos who act like they're God's gift to girls. Be real. Don't play games. You want someone to like you for who you are, not for someone you're trying to be.

Valuing and accepting yourself, dealing with the pathology of your past, making mature decisions, and developing your spiritual life are only a few of the ingredients that make a great mate. But once you've conquered these and feel you can play the dating game with good sense and God's wisdom, you're well on your way to finding your heart's desire. Someday, some special person is going to be mighty lucky to win your love.

SOMETHING TO THINK ABOUT . . .

- Of the four qualities that make a great mate mentioned in this chapter, which is your strongest area? Which is your weakest?
- Write down three things you will do this month to strengthen your weak area.
- Which of the dating guidelines comes naturally to you?
- What do you feel you need to work on?

---

1. Brenda Walsh and Kay Kuzma, Passionate Prayer Promises (Nampa, Idaho: Pacific Press® Publishing Association, 2008).

CHAPTER 6:
TANGLING WITH THE TEMPERAMENTS

Faye loves people. She is talkative and vivacious—the life of the party. Bob's friends envy him living with such a happy, spontaneous wife. But Bob doesn't think he is so lucky. Faye's forgetfulness and disorganization bug him. Why can't she just put her keys or glasses in one place so she can find them? And she is always missing appointments because she forgets to look at her calendar— that's if she has remembered to write it on the calendar in the first place.

Faye's feelings about Bob? She considers her perfectionistic husband an old stick-in-the-mud. He never has any fun. He is always picking things up, putting things away, filing, making lists, and methodically checking off each item. And no matter how much Faye teases and begs, he won't budge from his easy chair if it's his scheduled reading time. He is so organized—and so boring!

What's the problem in this marriage? Tangled temperaments!

Dori is a dynamic go-getter. She is a sharp real-estate agent who was promoted to branch manager before the end of her first year on the job. She has a special knack to see what needs to be done and has no trouble telling others what to do. This habit, however, spills over into her home life, and she ends up being a nagging wife.

But what else would you expect if you were married to Stanton? He never does anything! He just sits there watching TV. Nothing would ever get done around the home if it weren't for Dori—or so she thinks. Stanton is easygoing and enjoys a good time. And the more Dori nags, the more Stanton retreats and stubbornly does what he wants to do without informing his wife.

What went wrong in this relationship? Tangled temperaments!

What could help Faye and Bob, or Dori and Stanton? An understanding of the temperaments. A temperament is a natural disposition. It's an inborn behavioral style that permanently affects your manner of thinking, feeling, and acting—and it is reflected in your personality. Understanding the differences between the temperaments while you are still in this dating stage can save you from a mountain of adjustment problems during those first few years of marriage.

Can Temperaments Change?

Unlike interests, temperaments seldom, if ever, change. Change in behavior, of course, is always possible. This may make it appear that a person's basic temperament has changed, but this is probably not so.

For example, let's take Forgetful Faye. Faye may come to the realization that her forgetfulness is getting in the way of a positive relationship with her husband. An irresponsible reaction would be to lament, "Well, that's just the way I am. Take me or leave me!" Too often, that's exactly what happens. The spouse either resentfully chooses to remain married or decides it isn't worth it and leaves.

How much better it would be if Faye would choose to change her behavior. Realizing that she is not naturally organized and has a problem remembering things, Faye decides to purchase a large calendar and she hangs it next to the telephone. Every message is then written on that calendar. She also carries an appointment book with her, which she updates every morning before leaving the house. She makes a list of things she must do that day—items that need to be purchased and appointments that need to be kept. She also organizes her home so everything has a place, including her keys and glasses, and then she works hard to always put them there. Forgetfulness is still a natural part of her temperament, but she is not going to let it destroy her marriage.

Does Boring Bob have any responsibility to change? Of course he does. He can choose to deviate from his schedule when he realizes it would make Faye happy. Why not leave the mowing of the lawn one more day in order to take advantage of a seminar Faye would like to have him attend with her? It doesn't change his basic temperament, but his flexible behavior is a lot more fun to live with.

And what about Stanton and Dori? If Stanton continues to follow his natural inclination to take life easy and put things off until he feels like doing them, his temperament may cost him his marriage. Realizing that Dori is a natural boss who ends up nagging if things don't get done, Stanton has gotten in the habit of asking Dori every morning what she would like him to do that day. Together they go over the list of suggestions and decide on the feasibility of accomplishing these things in the next twenty-four hours. If there is a special on TV that evening, it is planned into their schedule so Stanton doesn't have to listen to Dori's nagging and feel guilty because he has chosen to watch it.

And what about Dori's nagging? Well, she knows that it comes naturally for her to tell others what to do, but she doesn't want to be a nag. Since, however, it is a long-term habit, she's going to need some help when she starts nagging. All Stanton has to say in a genuinely empathetic way is, "Sweetheart," and she gets the message and chooses to change her behavior.

Unless they are understood, accepted, and appreciated, temperaments can become tangled and strangle the life out of a marriage. And you'll find that very few couples are like Bob and Faye and Dori and Stanton. Not too many people modify their behavior after marriage. That's why it is important during the dating process to understand your own temperament and that of the person you love. Discuss your unique temperaments—and what bugs you about the other. If one person becomes defensive or is unwilling to discuss these differences, you shouldn't consider marriage yet.

If you truly love each other, you will want to work on some behavioral changes that might make your relationship more satisfying and might increase your chances for a fulfilling marriage. Determine together what changes you each would like to make and then keep your relationship on a dating basis long enough to see if these changes in behavior become permanent. If you are both comfortable with the persons you have become, you may be ready to consider engagement.

Just remember, it's only the behavior that has changed. Your basic temperaments have remained the same. Unless you can truly respect each other's basic temperaments, don't get married. These temperaments will continue to be exhibited throughout life in ways you can't even imagine right now. Even though changes seem to have been made during your courtship, there is no guarantee that they will continue to be made or that your partner won't revert to old habit patterns after marriage.

HOW KNOWING THE TEMPERAMENTS CAN HELP

The theory of temperaments is ancient. Hippocrates, who lived hundreds of years before Christ, was the first to write about temperaments and to make an effort to categorize them in some way. He observed four significantly different types of individuals with clusters of related behaviors. He named these temperament styles after different body fluids: sanguine (the happy, pleasure-loving person) was the Greek word for *blood;* phlegmatic (the easy-going, peace-loving, and sometimes indifferent individual) for phlegm; melancholy (the sensitive perfectionist who has a tendency toward sadness and depression) for black bile;

and choleric (the strong-willed and sometimes angry controller) for yellow bile.

When I first studied these temperaments, I was amazed to find that some psychologists still refer to such ancient thinking today. Also, I had a very difficult time accepting the idea that people could be put into boxes. Human behavior is much more complex than that. God's creativity is such that there have never been two individuals who were exactly the same—not even identical twins. How could people be so bold as to attempt to put a person's personality in a box?

Years later, my fourteen-year-old son, Kevin, and I were listening to some seminar tapes on the four temperaments. As Kevin listened to the description of the choleric person, he insightfully commented, "Mom, she's talking about Dad." I had to agree; the description of the choleric person, who sees what needs to be done and tells people what to do, did sound like the administrator I married. We laughed and I thought that was the end of it.

The next day, however, when choleric Dad came home from work, he greeted his phlegmatic son in the typical way, "Hi, Kev. Have you fed the dogs yet?" Kevin who usually resented his dad's reminders, came running to me with a big smile on his face, saying "Hey, Mom, my choleric dad is home!" Kevin's insight about his father's temperament helped him respect his dad for the way he was, rather than resent him because he wasn't as easygoing as his son.

Suddenly, I realized there might be something positive about this simplistic way of categorizing people. If a person could use this tool to better understand himself and the person he lives with, perhaps he could accept his mate's personality and behavior patterns easier. A person might also understand better how he himself could change in order to foster a more satisfying marriage relationship. And the earlier in the relationship a person gets this understanding, the better. So keep reading!

OPPOSITES ATTRACT

Understanding temperaments can be a helpful tool in the selection of a life partner. I'm sure you know by now that opposites attract—but opposites don't necessarily have an easy time living together.

Why do opposites attract? It's as if the weaknesses in one individual creates a void in his or her life, and finding a person who has those characteristics fills that void. If you really want to avoid tangling temperaments, it follows that one of the wisest things a young person can do before marriage is work on strengthening his or her own weak traits. When your own temperaments are balanced, you become less needy. Ideally this will increase your chances of being attracted to a person with more similar temperaments who would be easier to get along with.

If you know (or suspect) that you and the person you're serious about are opposites in personality, there are a few things you can do to avoid conflict.

First of all, *accept the fact that you're opposites*. If you truly respect each other, you can have a dynamic, exciting, passionate marriage and be totally opposite in temperaments. If you really care about each other, you won't try to make someone do things "your" way as if it's the only way. Instead, you will allow and encourage your loved one to be the person he or she was meant to be—for, after all, that's who you fell in love with!

Second, if you're opposites, be prepared to work harder to make sure your marriage doesn't become trapped in misunderstanding and resentment because of your differences. This may mean dialoguing each day about your growing relationship or reading books about communication and problem solving and putting the techniques you learn into practice. You may need to take marriage enrichment courses together, or even go for professional counseling if the going gets rough.

When I started writing this book, a friend came up to me and said, "Make sure you tell young lovers how difficult the first year of marriage is."

"What do you mean?" I asked.

"Well," my friend replied, "there are just so many adjustments you have to make in getting used to another person."

I thought about that statement. Of course, there are always adjustments to make in marriage. But it doesn't have to be difficult. No doubt the more similar two people are, the better they can understand each other once they're married. But opposites can learn to adjust as well. They'll just have to work at it a little more.

You make the choice. At least during these dating years, you can make a more informed choice by understanding the strengths and weaknesses of each other's temperaments and how one type of temperament might affect another. Then you can begin celebrating the strengths and working on the weaknesses. We'll spend the rest of the chapter looking at the dynamics of temperaments in a relationship.

DEFINING THE TEMPERAMENTS

Let's go back to Hippocrates and take a look at the four basic temperaments he described. As you read, remember that there is no such thing as a purely sanguine, phlegmatic, melancholy, or choleric person, so don't be concerned if you can't find yourself clearly in one category. We are all shades and blends of the various temperaments. In fact, the most balanced, and possibly the easiest to live with, may be a combination of all four. The important thing to consider is the weaknesses in each of these temperaments and then to work on overcoming them. It's one of the most important things you can do while you're still single in order to increase your chances of having healthy relationships in the future.

One more caution. Don't pigeonhole yourself in one of these categories and then use your natural temperament as an excuse for your behavior. You control your behavior. You don't have to be a slave to your temperament. You can change.

SANGUINE

Sanguines like to be the center of attention and have a good time. They do things for pleasure. Most sanguines are outgoing, talkative, friendly, optimistic, and curious. They also have a sense of humor, are childlike, somewhat forgetful, impulsive, and often controlled by circumstances, which may cause them to be irresponsible at times. They may get angry easily, but they don't usually hold grudges. They are the life of the party and enjoy being up front. They volunteer for jobs, spontaneously touch and inspire others, and are, in short, people-oriented. But their relationships may be based on a selfish motive, since sanguines crave an audience.

If you find yourself in this category, you may need to make the effort to think of others before yourself. Try making people feel special by remembering their names and birthdays, and by taking the time to really listen to others rather than doing all the talking yourself.

When you enthusiastically volunteer your time and talents, be sure you carry your fair share of responsibility. And stick to a project until it's finished—even though it may no longer be much fun. Learn to delegate when appropriate.

You may also need to start planning more so you will be better prepared for future events. If you spend a little more time getting organized and pay more attention to details, those around you will be happier.

Phlegmatic

The phlegmatic person is the peace-loving, conflict-avoiding observer. Other traits might include easygoing, relaxed, calm, patient, sympathetic, kind, compassionate, competent, steady, agreeable, not easily upset, quiet, observant, and inoffensive. Phlegmatics dislike change. They tend to keep their emotions to themselves and are good under pressure. They are easy to get along with, and because they take time to talk and listen, they usually have many friends.

If you are phlegmatic, you need to know that your laid-back attitude is often a source of irritation to others. You've got to learn to pull your fair share. Be observant about what needs to be done and don't put off doing it. Solve problems when they arise. Learn to talk through difficult situations rather than retreat from them. Share negative feelings instead of bottling them up. Show motivation and enthusiasm. Don't be afraid to try new things. Laugh, smile, and express positive emotion on a regular basis.

Melancholy

Are you a deep thinker? Do you have a perfectionistic bent? Are you deeply sensitive? Then you're probably a melancholy. Here's the textbook description of a melancholy: analytical, conscientious, idealistic, artistic, enjoys details and beautiful things. Melancholies are economical and self-sacrificing. Because they take things seriously, they are easily depressed, pessimistic, suspicious of others, and often moved to tears. They avoid attracting attention and are content to stay in the background. Melancholy people may be cautious when making friends, but they are devoted once they're in a relationship. They make good listeners and great helpers.

My advice to the melancholies: learn to enjoy every day. Try to be more spontaneous and do things that are pleasurable. Take the time to cultivate and enjoy more friendships.

Because melancholies have a tendency toward negative thinking, they must work on thinking positively. They need to work on counting their blessings and expressing thanks, while resisting the temptation to gossip and spread bad news. And because melancholies are usually perfectionists, they must make a concerted effort to accept themselves and others unconditionally.

Choleric

Cholerics are goal- or production-oriented, and they enjoy getting things done. It's not hard for cholerics to become workaholics. They are natural leaders and are good at delegating work and motivating others. Cholerics are unusually well-organized, confident, dynamic, active, strong-willed, independent, not easily discouraged, practical, impatient, unemotional and, at times, bossy, and controlling. The problem is, they are probably right! Cholerics enjoy controversy and seem to have little need for friends. They see in terms of the big picture and can figure out quickly what needs to be done. That's why they excel in emergencies.

If you are a choleric, you may need to make some changes that will make you easier to live with. Accept the fact that no one is perfect. Don't pressure others into your high-performance standard. Be willing to apologize and say, "I'm sorry," when you're wrong.

Learn to relax. Take time to make friends and to participate in fun activities. Cultivate patience by not expecting immediate solutions to everything. Encourage others' ideas and choices rather than constantly forcing your own.

When the Temperaments Tangle

Have you found the one or two (or maybe more) temperaments that sound like you? How about the person you're seriously dating? What is he or she like?

Now we'll take a look at what the potential problems might be if you were to marry someone of a different temperament. While none of these problems is insurmountable, you'll do yourselves a favor to talk about your personality differences before you make a lifetime commitment.

The sanguine and the choleric. The sanguine wants to have a good time while the choleric wants to get things done. The sanguine is impulsive, childlike, and forgetful while the choleric is organized, practical, and bossy. Can you see areas of possible conflict?

The sanguine and the melancholy. The sanguine says, "If we've got to do it, let's have fun!" The melancholy says, "If we do it, then let's do it right." They approach life from opposite ends of the spectrum which, ultimately, is the source of most of their conflicts.

The sanguine and the phlegmatic. The sanguine is impulsive and outgoing. The phlegmatic doesn't like to try new things and may be a bit introverted. And while the sanguine is talkative and willing to share feelings, the phlegmatic prefers to bottle up negative feelings and avoid problem-solving. These differences can easily cause misunderstandings.

The choleric and the melancholy. Because they both like to see things get done, the choleric and the melancholy may be more alike than some of the other temperaments. But they can tangle if the choleric is interested in the practical way to immediately get something done, and the melancholy insists on perfection regardless of how long it takes. When it comes to emotions, they could have a difficult time understanding each other since the choleric acts impatiently and is not easily discouraged while the melancholy is thorough, easily depressed, pessimistic, and suspicious.

The choleric and the phlegmatic. Here is a real potential for conflict. The choleric is a doer; the phlegmatic is not. The choleric leaves the house in the morning expecting that certain things will be accomplished by the phlegmatic. The phlegmatic happily spends his or her day on other pursuits—and never quite gets around to the choleric's agenda. Too often this leads to nagging, bossy behavior from the choleric. The phlegmatic isn't as open about feelings and so tries to avoid conflict by not saying anything. Over the years internal resentment begins to build, and before the choleric/phlegmatic couple realizes it, the phlegmatic's affection has turned to hostility. Once this happens, it is very difficult to restore the original love relationship.

And look out when the wife is a choleric who naturally assumes a leadership position while the husband feels that even though he is a phlegmatic, he should be the head of the household. This couple is heading for rough waters.

Mutual respect is the stuff that holds a choleric/phlegmatic marriage together. Without it, a couple is doomed to a relationship gone cold due to harbored resentment and anger.

The melancholy and the phlegmatic. While melancholies and phlegmatics both have more introverted personalities, there are some basic differences. First of all, their attitudes may conflict. The phlegmatic is usually more positive, and the melancholy tends to be pessimistic.

Another conflict might arise in regards to how things are done. The melancholy is extremely conscientious, paying attention to details and making sure things are done right. The phlegmatic couldn't care less. Can you see the melancholy partner following around the phlegmatic, picking up after him and retouching projects that the phlegmatic considered done? I can almost hear the melancholy complain, "Can't you ever do anything right?" And if you listen carefully, you could hear the phlegmatic lament, "Why can't you just accept me the way I am?"

Marrying someone with a different temperament can make life interesting. Just make sure you date each other over a long enough period of time, and see each other in as many different situations as possible, so you have a pretty good idea about how your temperaments mesh and be willing to accept and respect those differences.

When Jan and I got married, I was ignorant of our different temperaments and how they might affect our relationship. I did know he was very methodical and organized and that he wouldn't think of starting his day without a list. In my book, lists were for letting people know what you wanted for Christmas, not for organization!

After marriage we got along just fine as long as he didn't tell his impulsive, disorganized, and fun-loving wife what to do. In fact, our differences in temperaments didn't really tangle until the children came along. I felt Jan unfairly blamed me when I didn't make the children do everything he had listed for them to do. I resented him for being too hard on the kids and then punishing me for their disobedience. *After all,* I thought, *if he asked them to do something, it was his responsibility to make sure they did it, not mine.*

The crisis came one Friday night. I had been blamed one time too many, and he was utterly frustrated with the wife he couldn't control. I stood up and said, "Enough. I'd rather live alone than be constantly blamed for something that wasn't my fault and then be manipulated by your anger." He was shocked. He had no idea I felt so strongly about it, and he certainly hadn't meant to hurt me. He was only doing what he felt was necessary to keep his family organized and help his wife be a better mother.

That night was a major turning point in our acceptance of each other's differences. By openly sharing how deeply we felt, we gained a better understanding of why we did the things we did. The result? Our respect for each other deepened and our expectations became more realistic.

You can't avoid all the temperament tangles in marriage, but the more you can grow to accept and respect each other's differences before marriage, the fewer tangles there will be after.

SOMETHING TO THINK ABOUT . . .

- What temperament category do you find yourself in? What about the person you're dating?
- Make a list of ways in which you find your personalities compatible.
- Now list the areas of potential conflict.
- Do your areas of conflict outweigh the areas of compatibility?
- How will you use your understanding of the temperaments to help diffuse your next argument?

Chapter 7:
Enjoying the Single Life

I vividly remember my college days and the frustration of liking guys who never glanced my way, the awkwardness of tactfully trying to get out of dates with guys who wouldn't take No for an answer—and the agony of waiting. Waiting for a phone call for a Saturday evening date (it didn't come). Waiting for that handsome man to walk me to class (he walked my best friend instead).

Even after I was happily married, I had recurring nightmares of not dating or of watching the man with whom I was madly in love pay fond attention to someone else. This may not sound like the subject matter of most nightmares, but I assure you these dreams were every bit as terrifying. I experienced heart-wrenching agony because I was not able to catch the man of my dreams.

If it weren't for those recurring nightmares, I might have forgotten the fear of rejection that is often part of the dating years. For many it is agony. But rest assured, you are not the only one who has suffered. The fear of not being able to find the right marriage partner is a common one. And not even popularity, good looks, or money can shield you from these feelings. However, don't let those feelings ruin this special time in your life.

Being single can hold unique opportunities. You may even find that once you get involved doing what you've always had a desire to do, you actually *enjoy* your single status. And in the process you'll meet some fascinating people, and you'll give yourself the chance to meet the right person for you. Here are some ideas on how to make the best use of this special time in your life.

Get Involved in Group Activities

Avoid becoming a recluse. Don't talk yourself into staying home, convincing yourself that you would rather read a good book than be out doing something with someone else. Make yourself sign up for the beach party, cheer for your school's team, join the choir, or become a member of the ski club.

Join a singles' group. This is a great way to get acquainted with interesting people. If your church doesn't have a singles' group, why not start one? Or you may want to check into other churches in your community and join an established group.

I admit it's not always easy getting involved in group activities, especially when you think everyone else in the group has a special friend and you don't. But if you'll crank up your self-worth and get involved, you'll soon find that there are quite a number of singles searching for friends who are also frightened of being alone in a group.

CULTIVATE FRIENDSHIPS

Every friendship (both male and female) adds something to your growth and personal understanding. Great marriage partners usually have a wide variety of friends who have taught them a lot about the importance of sharing interests, developing new skills, getting along with different personalities, communicating feelings and needs, and unselfishly giving time and attention to others—all important lessons that prepare a person for marriage.

However, don't limit yourself by thinking every friend has to be marriage material. In fact, not every person you may go someplace with has to be screened for mate potential. Casual "dating" is an important way to cultivate friendships of all types—and an important precursor to more serious dating. Perhaps it should be called "appointment making" rather than dating. After all, you don't consider it a "date" when you call someone and say, "Hey, haven't seen you in a long time. What about lunch?" I believe marriages would be happier if more of this type of friendship cultivation went on prior to serious dating.

Too many young people miss so much in life because they are afraid to cultivate various types of friendships. They are so busy hunting for their one and only that they miss the blessings of good friends along the way.

SAY YES

Craig was one of the most popular guys on campus. The Sadie Hawkins banquet was coming up where girls asked guys, and Craig thought Sheila might ask him. She was popular and talented, and they had a good time joking together in chemistry lab.

One day, however, as Craig walked out of the cafeteria, he heard a faint voice behind him. It was Rhoda. "Craig, ah, I mean," Rhoda stammered, "I was wondering if you'd go to the banquet with me."

Rhoda was not Craig's type. Other than attend class, she didn't participate in school activities. She was shy. Her straight brown hair, plain features, and sometimes unkempt appearance did not make her especially appealing.

"Well, I don't know, Rhoda," he hesitated. "You caught me by surprise. I really don't know . . ."

Craig saw a look of disappointment cross Rhoda's face. How could he do this to her? It must have taken a lot of courage for Rhoda to ask him. Why shouldn't he go with her? He had no real reason to say No, other than his own selfish desire. But he had two big reasons to say Yes. It would make Rhoda happy, and she had asked him first.

"Rhoda," he said at last, "I'd be happy to go."

His buddies couldn't believe it. When they started to tease, he cut them short. He wouldn't allow Rhoda to be demeaned. On the evening of the banquet, Rhoda looked lovely, especially with the beautiful corsage Craig had given her. She held her head high and smiled. They had a good time getting acquainted. Though they never dated again, both gained a new friend that evening.

When I first heard this story, I thought that's probably what Christ would have done. In fact, Jesus attended a banquet where a woman with a questionable reputation, a former prostitute, wanted to anoint Him with perfume. He could have easily pushed her away, like Simon wanted Him to do, but Christ thought more of the feelings of others than about His own reputation. He allowed this woman to show her appreciation in this way rather than embarrassing her by refusing her attentions. Why not follow Christ's example and say Yes to an appointment to make someone happy?

"But if I say Yes once," I can hear you saying, "won't the person keep bugging me to say Yes again?" Not if you make it clear that you want to be a friend, not a date.

ENJOY BEING SINGLE

Acting as if you're desperate to get married is a good way to scare off potential dates. Too many single people waste what should be the best years of their lives plotting and planning how they can snag the best marriage partner. Then they spend the next half a century singing the jingle:

I wish I were single again, again.
I wish I were single again.
For if I were single, my pockets would jingle,
I wish I were single again.

Marriage will come in God's time. Listen to those who have traveled this road before; they will tell you it is far better being single than being married to the wrong person.

So enjoy yourself. Take every day as it comes along, and make the most of it as you cultivate your own skills and interests. You'll be a much more desirable date if you approach life with this attitude—and a much, much more desirable mate.

Serve Others

The worst thing you can do while you're single is to feel sorry for yourself. Avoid thoughts of self-pity. Reach outside yourself and serve others. Your problems will seem small, indeed, when you start getting involved with others—especially those who really need you.

Have you ever considered mission service? There are hundreds of exotic places (and some not so exotic) that could benefit greatly by your willingness to serve. Kim, my daughter, spent a summer in Paris volunteering at the Country Life Restaurant, a Christian witnessing program in the heart of the city. Kevin taught third-graders on the island of Majuro for a year—and got in some great surfing too. You might prefer working with an agricultural project in Africa, building a church school in Palau, or sailing with a mission boat which provides medical care to the tribes along the Amazon.

If you don't like to travel, there are many closer-to-home places to serve. What about the local day-care center, hospital, nursing home, hospice, library, nonprofit ministry, or Christian radio station? And there are hundreds of volunteer jobs just waiting to be filled in local churches.

When you get involved serving others, a wonderful thing happens—you forget about yourself. In addition, you meet some very interesting people in some of the most unlikely places.

Do the Things You Have Always Wanted to Do

Too many people get married thinking that marriage will automatically fill their cup of unfulfilled dreams to overflowing. That seldom happens.

Use the time that you're single to do the things you have always wanted to do. There are many things that may be much easier to do now than after you've made a commitment to someone else.

Have you ever wanted to travel? Do it. There are many young adults who travel in small groups and camp throughout Europe, sail the Caribbean, travel the Orient, or join an archeological dig in the Middle East. If this is your dream, begin talking about it with your friends, read everything you can find about it in the library or on the Internet, call a travel agency, or check the colleges and universities and ask about their summer tour programs and their field study courses.

One Christmas when we were camping in the Virgin Islands, a group of students from Michigan State University were there studying ecology. What a great way to spend Christmas vacation! And my daughter, Kari, took advantage of a summer tour to the Holy Land and received twelve units of credit from her university.

Where there is a will, there is a way. Now is the time to make your dreams come true. And what a much more interesting person you will be to your friends in the future because of your travel experiences.

What about taking another degree or enroll in a specialized training course in an interesting avocation? Don't wait. My heart goes out to young couples who marry before they finish their career training. When one or both are trying to juggle night classes, a job, and a family, it's a wonder they can maintain their sanity. And if kids happen along unexpectedly, they might as well try climbing Mount Everest in a wheelchair. Right now, while you are single, may be your window of opportunity to complete the education and training you desire. Go for it!

What if you've finished your training and are established in your career? Now is a great time to pursue hobbies and develop your talents that aren't necessarily used on the job. Take drama classes and be a part in a local theatrical production. Join a community choir or orchestra and develop your musical ability. Paint, sculpt, build furniture, make quilts. The sky is the limit. And in the process you'll likely meet some very interesting people.

START A SELF-IMPROVEMENT COURSE

No one is so beautiful, talented, intelligent, or polite that he or she couldn't benefit by a self-improvement course. Assess yourself. What could you do to improve yourself? It may help to talk to your best friends or a trusted teacher or counselor and get his or her input.

Do you want to make a change in your physical appearance? Have color analysis done to determine what colors look best on you. Get your hair styled. Join an exercise class and tone up your muscles. Lose weight—or gain it. Go shopping with someone who can help you select a couple outfits that make you look your best. If there is something you really don't like about your appearance and it can be changed, go for a makeover. It's never too late to get those crooked teeth straightened or to have plastic surgery, if you feel this would make you happier about the way you look.

Just remember that what you are in your heart is ultimately more important than how you look. If your "insides" are attractive, they'll add a beauty to your physical appearance that can't be matched by any improvement you do on the outside.

Are you looking for ways to improve your personality? Dale Carnegie's classic book *How to Win Friends and Influence People* is a good beginning. And while you are at it, why don't you pick up a good etiquette book? Social know-how will help you feel more comfortable in various group situations. Take the time to learn how to be a great conversationalist. Develop communication skills that will put others at ease and make them feel they are the most important people in the world. If you can do that for people, they will think you are pretty terrific.

DEVELOPING DOMESTIC SKILLS

Getting married and establishing a home requires the development of certain skills that aren't necessarily taught in school. Bone up on domestic skills now.

Don't make the mistake of equating domestic skills with woman's work. You may fall in love with a woman who volunteers happily to clean house if you do the cooking and laundry. Or your husband may expect you to help earn the family income while he shares child-rearing responsibilities. More and more couples are finding that stereotyped roles just don't meet their individual needs. Most women today have career training, and most men admit they want to be vitally involved in their children's lives. So whether you're male or female, you'll find it to your advantage to develop your domestic skills.

Do you know how to cook creative and nutritious meals? Are you comfortable entertaining guests? A good course in nutrition or a vegan cooking class may be one of the best investments you'll ever make.

Have you had experience doing the laundry, removing stains, and ironing shirts? Do you know how to make beds with mitered corners, clean the bathroom tile, or shampoo a carpet? And how knowledgeable are you when it comes to the basic maintenance and repair of a car?

Are you comfortable with children? This is an essential skill for both male and female. Start with a good child development course and then supplement your knowledge with real experience. Offer to babysit for friends, or volunteer in the church nursery or a day-care program. You may want to homeschool your children someday. Will you be prepared? Perhaps you could volunteer at the local elementary school or take a few education courses.

Do you know how to make and follow a budget? Do you understand your insurance needs and know how to figure your taxes? What about savings and investments?

In time you will need all these skills. Why not get a head start and learn as much as you can about establishing a home and family now.

ESTABLISH A CLOSER RELATIONSHIP WITH CHRIST

If you're lonely, make Jesus your constant companion. Your dynamic relationship with Him will cushion heartache, rejection, and all the other negative emotions you might suffer while you're single.

Lean on His promises. He says that if you will trust in Him, He will give you the desires of your heart (Psalm 37:3, 4). I can't think of anything more reassuring than that, can you? Remember, God's timetable is perfect. You don't need to be anxious.

Every minute you invest in developing your relationship with Christ is time well spent. The fruit of the Spirit found in Galatians 5:22 (love, joy, peace, long-suffering, kindness, goodness, faithfulness, gentleness, self-control), which are a byproduct of a dynamic relationship with Jesus, is the best marriage insurance policy you could have.

There are many good Bible studies available to help you mature and grow in the Lord. Visit your local Christian bookstore and look for titles dealing with spiritual leadership, personal discipline, servanthood, or love. Go online.

Visit www.bibleinfo.com. Through your study you'll discover what makes a good Christian husband and wife.

Finally, memorize Jeremiah 29:11–13, "For I know the plans I have for you, says the Lord. They are plans for good and not for evil, to give you a future and a hope. In those days when you pray, I will listen. You will find me when you seek me, if you look for me in earnest" (TLB).

AVOID THE HAZARDS OF THE SINGLE LIFE

With all the joys and opportunities that the single life holds, there are some dangers, especially if you are not satisfied with dating—or waiting. When your desires for a home and family go unfulfilled for a long period of time, you may be tempted to compromise your standards. I'd like to encourage you to hold out for God's best, and beware of the hazards that may cause you to settle for less.

Hazard #1: *You date someone with a questionable character because you are beginning to lose hope that the right one will ever appear.*

It's entirely possible that your expectations to find a perfect mate are unreasonably high and that you may need to readjust your thinking. Marriage means living with another human being—not with an angel. But, there are certain standards you should not compromise just because you are lonely. For example, do you want to be married so badly that you're willing to date someone who has a substance-abuse problem, or someone who promises to make needed changes in his of her life only to come up with excuses when there are no results?

Only you will be able to decide what ideals you don't want to compromise. After all, you will be the one who will have to spend your life living with this person.

Hazard #2: *You are pressured into a sexual relationship thinking that it will encourage the person you are dating to make a permanent commitment to you.*

I hope you hear these next three words. It never works. IT NEVER WORKS. Trust me, if the person you love were willing to make a lifetime commitment, he or she wouldn't ask for sex outside of that commitment.

Hazard #3: *You rush into a marriage thinking it may be your last chance.*

Even if you are convinced that you are truly in love and your boyfriend or girlfriend is everything you want a mate to be, it never pays to rush a good thing. Enjoy each day of your courtship. Make your plans wisely. If it's truly love, and not just passionate desire, it will last. And if you have any doubts about the relationship, that's even more reason to take your time. Too many people who have felt they have waited long enough, jump into a marriage, and then find themselves wishing they were single again.

The important thing is to enjoy your single life and use this time that God has given you to do what you feel called to do. And who knows who might walk into your life. When you least expect it, a rather ordinary day may become your "enchanted evening."

SOMETHING TO THINK ABOUT . . .

- List the pros and cons of your single status.
- If you were to stay single for the next few years, what do you think you might like to do that might be different from what you're doing now?
- What would be the first step on that journey?
- Make a covenant with the Lord today to earnestly pray about what He would have you do during this period of your life.

CHAPTER 8:
HOW TO BREAK UP AND REMAIN FRIENDS

A pilot of a single-engine plane once turned to his three passengers and announced that the engine had failed and they were going to crash. Their only hope was to bail out. But there were only three parachutes on board and the pilot planned to take one. After the pilot jumped, one of the passengers explained to the other two that he was a famous scientist and considered by some to be one of the brightest men in the world. "I owe it to society," he said, "to take a parachute and jump." And he did, leaving an old man and a Boy Scout.

The old man sadly looked at the youth. "Sonny," he said, "I've lived a good long life. You take that last parachute." Tears came to his eyes.

The Boy Scout replied, "Sir, you don't have to cry. The brightest man in the world just grabbed my knapsack and jumped."

You know what I learned from this story? Don't grab a knapsack when you need a parachute!

No one enters a serious dating relationship anticipating a breakup. You expect fun, companionship, and romance. When romance is on the rise, there is an exhilarating feeling that nothing could ever go wrong. *But it can.* The element of romance seldom lasts forever. In that gray area between romantic illusion and true love, breaking up is a real possibility.

If you're seriously dating, you are at high risk to suffer the hurt and alienation caused by a breakup. When a breakup occurs, you're going to need more than a knapsack to get you safely down from the romantic heights to the solid ground of reality. It's a bitter fall to the depths of rejection.

To make it safely, without incurring psychological scars that may last for months or years, you're going to need a parachute. In fact, you may need more than one. Without them, you could find your hopes dashed to pieces, your dreams turned to nightmares and your desires drowned in depression.

Parachute 1: Discover How Dating Behavior Relates to Breaking Up

The first parachute you need is information on how to develop dating relationships in such a way that the risk of painfully breaking up is minimized. A lot has to do with your philosophy of making friends with the opposite sex. Here's a healthy attitude: go into a friendship for the experience. Discuss up front that if at any time one of you feels that this relationship isn't what you really want, then each of you has the right to say, "OK, this isn't quite right. It's just not working for us." Enjoy the friendship for the *now*. Celebrate the fact that you have grown and know yourself better because of it. It has made you more aware of what you want and don't want in a lasting relationship. With this attitude, the fall may not be so devastating.

The key is to keep the getting-to-know-you period of dating on a friendship level for as long as possible. Once you begin adding the romantic elements of caressing embraces and long, passionate kisses, the danger of suffering the psychological pain of a breakup is significantly increased.

An age-old principle is that the higher you fly, the farther you have to fall and the greater the pain upon impact. As you are building a relationship, it is wise to keep your physical involvement to a minimum through the casual dating stage. When you follow this course, it is relatively easy to move from one relationship to another, making friends, having fun and enjoying the association of a wide variety of individuals, without breaking hearts and crying bitter tears when you move on.

Friends are special commodities. They are what make life rich and rewarding. The more time you invest in a relationship, the more you experience together, the more you share in common, the greater the chances are that you would enjoy this person's friendship on a long-term basis, regardless of who you marry. What a shame to feel that you can't continue to be friends with people you once dated just because they weren't right for marriage.

A breakup does not need to signal the end of a friendship. You can break up and still remain good friends if you haven't become too involved physically. In fact, it's good to discuss this possibility early in a friendship. "No matter how long this lasts, could we still be friends afterward?"

I've often joked that you should never make enemies of old boy- or girlfriends because you never know when you might need them in the future. Case in point: we were repairing the barbed wire fencing around my parents' mountain property in Colorado. The wire suddenly snapped and tore a deep gash in my daughter's boyfriend's finger. I took one look and knew the cut needed stitches. We were miles from an emergency center, and since the young man was from Canada, I didn't know if his insurance would cover the cost of medical care.

I was wondering what to do when I thought of my old boyfriend, who was a well-known surgeon with a medical practice about twenty miles away. I called for help, "Don, this is Kay. Would you mind sewing up my daughter's boyfriend's finger?" He did it—and without a fee.

Friends are important. Conduct your dating in such a way that the friends you go out with can be kept for a lifetime.

PARACHUTE 2: AVOID BECOMING INVOLVED IN RELATIONSHIPS YOU DON'T WANT TO CONTINUE

It's your choice whether or not a relationship continues. Avoid getting involved with someone who has a negative effect on you, someone who makes you feel bad. Don't continue dating anyone who puts you down, treats you disrespectfully, or is verbally or physically abusive. Don't kid yourself into thinking this person is the only fish in the sea so you have to put up with hurtful behavior if you want someone to date. Cut off the relationship before you become emotionally attached, saving yourself and the other party a lot of grief.

Also, avoid becoming involved with someone you don't want as a close friend. Don't lead a person on just because you want to be nice and don't know how to turn him or her down gracefully. Learn to say no early in the friendship. It's not fair to play games with another person's emotions just to see what you can get out of the relationship. It's cruel to use people for your own means.

Jane did this. She dated Stan primarily because his folks had money, and she enjoyed water skiing with him and going to their mountain cabin on the weekends. Before she knew it, Stan was madly in love with her, but she didn't have the same feelings. A breakup was inevitable.

Just because you don't want to date someone, doesn't mean that person can't be your friend. Many men and women have established quality friendships with each other without pressuring each other into a dating relationship.

The problem arises when you meet someone who is so anxious for a dating relationship that the minute anyone shows them any kindness, they immediately think that person is interested in something more serious than a friendship.

The answer isn't to be unfriendly and avoid these individuals. The answer is to be truthful—specifically truthful—about what you want from the relationship. Tell him, "I just want to be your friend." You may have to say something more specific, "I'd like to be your friend, but nothing more. Please don't call me at home, and don't ask me for a date."

If this type of person does ask you for a date, it's not wrong to say No. Neither is it wrong to go with him or her once, especially when you know it will make the person happy. But be truthful right up front: "I am saying Yes because I think we can have a good time together. I am not interested in a dating relationship, so let's just be friends. If you ask me again, I will say No. We don't have to date to be friends."

Parachute 3: Learn to Break Up Gracefully

When you become convinced that a dating relationship is not what you want, you must take the responsibility of ending it. How you do this will either destroy the chances of having this person as a friend in the future, or leave the door of friendship open. You will probably want to maintain his or her friendship, unless the person had a negative influence on your life, or he or she won't take No for an answer. Try following these guidelines for success:

1: Don't lead someone on when you want out.

It is not easy to break up. Some people don't want to hurt the other person, so they continue dating, rather than facing the situation. They may even begin treating their date in a negative way, hoping the person will get the hint and want out of the relationship just as badly. Some people, however, never seem to catch on. Sooner or later, you will have to break up. Prolonging the pain by treating the person disrespectfully is a mean thing to do.

2: Be sensitive to the timing of the breakup.

Don't decide to break up on the day your girlfriend flunks her history exam, or on the anniversary of the death of your boyfriend's father. If you know this breakup is going to be emotionally painful for the other person, it might be thoughtful to choose a time when he or she will have other friends available who can be supportive. Although there is never a "good" time for a breakup, use your common sense. Break the bad news gently at the best possible time.

3: DON'T SAY TOO MUCH.

Be truthful—but not brutally truthful. You don't have to try and justify why you want to break up by giving a speech on 101 Reasons I Don't Want to Date You Anymore. Many of your reasons may appear shallow to the person being rejected. And it's too easy to get sidetracked and argue over insignificant matters. Just clearly state your reason for wanting to break up in such a way that arguing is unnecessary:

- I am no longer happy in this relationship.
- I feel our differences are too great to have a lasting relationship.
- I have a desire to date other people.
- I'm too young and immature to settle down into a steady dating relationship.

Note: Each one of these reasons started with the word *I*. That brings me to the next point.

4: GIVE I-MESSAGES, NOT YOU-MESSAGES.

An I-message means the sender is taking responsibility for the breakup of the relationship, while a you-message casts blame on the other person. Notice the difference between, I am not happy when we are together, and I often go home feeling hurt, versus, You say things that hurt my feelings.

5: BREAK UP FACE-TO-FACE.

The breakup will be easier to accept if you at least have the guts to face the person you are breaking up with. Facing the person shows respect. Breaking up over the telephone, where you can discuss the situation together, is the next best way. Avoid a "Dear John" letter or e-mail, unless there is no possible way to get together or call. And don't ask someone to do your dirty work for you. Can you imagine how it makes the other person feel when he or she hears about your plans to break up from an acquaintance?

6: Be thoughtful.

It's not a bad idea to cushion your breakup by telling the other person what the relationship has meant to you. Mention a few of the person's admirable traits: I have really valued our friendship and love your sense of humor. I want to be your friend, but I don't want to continue dating.

Knowing that things are not going well in a relationship can help a person get prepared psychologically for the inevitable. Therefore, it may be thoughtful to warn your steady about a possible breakup. But don't keep threatening and then do nothing about it. No one enjoys a yo-yo existence—up one day and down the next. Be decisive. In the long run it's the least painful way.

If you want to keep a friend but end a dating relationship, be considerate and cushion the blow as much as possible. Remember the golden rule to treat others as you would want to be treated.

7: Don't spread gossip and cast blame in order to justify yourself.

The world doesn't need to know all the reasons you chose to end this relationship. Keep negative things to yourself. You don't have to justify your course of action by demeaning the other person. When you are asked about what happened, tell your story in such a way that it casts the best possible light on other person you broke up with. When a former boyfriend or girlfriend learns that you still think he or she is an OK person, it soothes the hurt feelings.

8: Don't avoid each other after a breakup.

When you see your ex, don't look the other way. Wave, say "hi," or stop and say a few words, even if it's about the weather. But be careful not to be so friendly that it gives the other person the message that you are sorry for the breakup and want to get back together again.

At the time of a breakup, the feelings of hurt and rejection may be so strong that you part without having said all that is on your mind. Arranging a time to talk when feelings are not so raw can bring the relationship to a more acceptable and satisfying close. This will help salvage the friendship and give you a better understanding of each other.

When Bev broke up with Jeff, he was devastated. Afraid he was going to cry, he walked out and slammed the door behind him, while she was trying to explain. Afterward, he was sorry for the way he acted, but was afraid to apologize for fear she would think he was trying to get back together. He was relieved when he got an e-mail from Bev. "Jeff, you've been a good friend, and I've enjoyed the time we've spent talking. When I broke up with you, we were both so emotionally upset that we never had a chance to close this stage of our relationship on a positive note. I'd like to do that—if you're willing. What about meeting me at Taco Bell next Wednesday at noon? Let me know if you can make it. This is not to get back together—just a time to talk. Bev."

Even if you are the one breaking up, you may find it difficult seeing your old girlfriend or boyfriend with someone new. But it's going to happen sooner or later, so get ready with a smile and a friendly "hi." It may be an act at first, but you'll find your feelings of attachment fading. Time is a wonderful healer.

Seeing your friend with someone else may cause you to realize just how much you really do care for that person. Sort through your feelings carefully. It may have been a good decision to end the relationship because of your incompatibility, your emotional dependence, or the negative influence you were having on each other. The feelings you experience when seeing your ex with someone else may merely be jealousy (someone has moved in on what you had considered your territory) or anger (your friend cared so little for you that he or she could immediately jump into another relationship). Examine your feelings before rushing to the phone and telling your former boyfriend or girlfriend that the breakup was a mistake.

9: Prayer can be a part of a breakup, but don't misuse it.

Avoid preaching at the other person or trying to sanctify your actions when you pray. When you say goodbye to a relationship, it is not out of hand to pause and say, "What's happening right now is painful to both of us. Let's just ask the Lord to lead us in the way we should go." Ask a special blessing on the person you are breaking up with, that the hurts will heal, and God will lead that person to a very special relationship in the future.

Parachute #4: How to React When Someone Breaks Up With You

Now, let's turn the tables. You will not always be the one doing the breaking up. What if you don't want a relationship to end, but your boyfriend or girlfriend is calling it quits? If you want to save face, heal quickly and ideally save a friend for the future, here are some important things *not* to do.

1: DON'T FALL APART.

Instead, take a deep breath. Smile, even though faintly, and calmly say, "I was hoping our relationship could grow into a long-term one. I respect you and your wishes, and I hope we can remain friends. I know God has someone special for both of us, and the most important thing is to allow Him to lead us." This speech can blow the other person away—and cement a friendship (not a courting relationship) for life. You don't have to part enemies.

If at the time of the breakup you are too hurt or angry to react calmly, try to avoid saying something you'll regret later. It's better to keep quiet and ask for some time to process what you've heard than to react violently and alienate your friend.

2: DON'T DO SOMETHING FOOLISH.

A breakup is not the end of the world, regardless of how you feel. You may feel like quitting your job, flunking out of school, falling into the arms (or bed) of someone else, marrying on the rebound, running away, getting drunk, or jumping off a cliff. But don't. Your feelings of rejection are temporary. Don't do something impulsive that may alter your life significantly.

Unconsciously you may feel that if you do something traumatic, your old boyfriend or girlfriend will feel sorry for you and come back. This seldom happens. Instead, your foolish actions are a message that you are an unstable person and the breakup was probably a good idea.

3: DON'T TURN BITTER.

The last thing you should do is try and get back at the person who has rejected you with what I call psychological murder. Words said at the time of breakup can be deadly. No matter how hurt and angry you may be, if you say hateful things and assassinate your ex's character, it's almost impossible to resurrect a friendship.

Revengeful feelings and actions have a tendency to boomerang, and you may end up being the person hurt most deeply.

4: Don't beg.

"Oh, John, I just can't live without you. You mean everything to me. Please, let's try again. Please, please, please. . . ." That's a great way to drive an even bigger wedge into your friendship. If that's your attitude, your old boyfriend may end up going to great lengths to avoid you. Your girlfriend may spread the word that you're a poor loser—and no one wants to date, let alone marry, a loser. No matter what you think, you can live without that person. You may be so in love that you don't think you can—*but you can.* Keep telling yourself that. You're far too valuable to God, your family, and your friends to fall apart just because one person rejected you.

5. Don't isolate yourself after a breakup.

Rejection makes you want to hide from others who may ask questions or feel sorrow for you. But when you're hurting, you need friends who will support you. Allow your friends to comfort you and to be a sounding board for your feelings.

While you'll need to spend some time alone to sort out your feelings, just as soon as possible, get yourself back into society. Do things you enjoy. Keep busy. Set new life goals, and move decisively in that direction. Step out and get involved in helping others. Healing will come much more quickly this way.

6: Don't be ashamed to grieve over your loss.

The more serious your relationship—the more deeply bonded you were to each other—the more painful a breakup will be, and the more time you will need to grieve. During this time you may go through four different stages in your grieving process. At first, you may deny that the breakup is actually happening: He's just infatuated with this other girl and will return to me, or It's just her time of the month. In a week or so, things will be OK.

As it dawns on you that this breakup is real, you may experience anger toward the person who has caused you pain. Here's where you have to guard yourself carefully so you don't do something foolish in an attempt to get back at that person.

In the third stage of grief, you'll feel like blaming yourself for what happened. You'll have a tendency to think, *If only.* . . . You may need to discuss your feelings with others so they can help you sort out the reality of the situation from your irrational thoughts. Talk about what you did or didn't do to cause the breakup. Don't blame yourself unnecessarily; this will only add feelings of guilt to your load of grief. This time of reflection can be a learning experience to help you avoid suffering from future rejection.

Finally, grief finishes its work when you realize and accept your breakup. Probably the best thing you can do when the full impact of your loss hits you is to have yourself a good long cry. Sob your heart out. It will really help. It's as if your tears wash away the hurt and pain within.

During this grieving period look for comfort in the Scriptures. Start with passages such as Psalm 23, Psalm 27 or Psalm 121. When your life seems darkest, remember these promises: "Weeping may endure for a night, / But joy comes in the morning" (Psalm 30:5), or, "The Lord is near to those who have a broken heart" (Psalm 34:18).

Afterward take three deep breaths and a cold shower, get dressed in your favorite outfit, splash on your most expensive cologne, and tackle the world. It's yours.

7: DON'T JUMP IMMEDIATELY INTO ANOTHER RELATIONSHIP.

The more serious your relationship, the more pain the breakup will cause, and the more time you will need to heal. Breakup time can be very vulnerable time. Because you are used to being close to another person, you now crave closeness. It's easy to fall into the trap of quickly becoming involved with someone else—anyone else. And without realizing what you're doing, you escalate the relationship into fast forward through the friendship phase to the physical involvement stage of your past relationship. History is filled with horror stories that are the result of relationships on the rebound. There's enough human misery in the world; you don't have to make a personal contribution.

8: DON'T PUNISH YOURSELF.

Rejection causes feelings of self-doubt and sometimes self-hate. Don't fall into the trap of equating your value with whether you can hold a relationship together. Consider how God values you. Because He made you and died for you, He values you supremely. In fact, He's crazy about you. (Review the Scriptures given in chapter 6.)

To help you through this period of self-blame, you may have to practice what is called self-talk. Tell yourself all the good things about yourself—and say these things over and over. Don't allow your mind to engage in negative self-criticism. That will just pull you downhill into depression, and the devil will rejoice.

If you feel there was truth in some of the accusations made against you that caused this breakup, it might be helpful to find a good counselor to give you a set of personality tests and then help you smooth off the rough edges of your personality that's causing others to reject you. Instead of punishing yourself, learn from this experience, so you don't have to continue suffering in the future from failed relationships.

9: DON'T BEGIN A SMEAR CAMPAIGN AGAINST THE OTHER PERSON.

Avoid treating the person as you think he or she deserves to be treated. Instead, turn the tables and say something kind. Here's some good counsel from Proverbs: "If your enemy is hungry, give him food! If he is thirsty, give him something to drink! This will make him feel ashamed of himself, and God will reward you" (25:21, 22, TLB).

Breaking up is hard, no matter what side you're on. In most cases, feelings of guilt and sadness accompany this decision. Why not do the unexpected and say something nice about the other person? I have a feeling it will surprise him or her, and you will probably find that your feelings of rejection will heal faster when bathed in a positive spirit.

10: DON'T GIVE UP GOD.

Many people testify, especially after a marriage breakup, that the only thing that got them through was their relationship with the Lord. Now is the time to lean on Him. Let His Spirit talk to you and minister to your needs. Search for Bible promises. Memorize them. And when the devil tempts you to become discouraged, fall back on one of God's promises, such as, "Be delighted with the Lord. Then he will give you all your heart's desires" (Psalm 37:4, TLB). It might also help to remember that "all things work together for good to those who love God" (Romans 8:28).

By now you are probably thinking, *I could never react to a breakup in a manner that cool, calm, and collected. I could never react with such understanding.* That's because most of us allow our feelings to dictate our actions. Breaking up causes feelings of guilt, alienation, rejection, and revenge, and too often without realizing it, actions follow. God's way is the opposite. The apostle Paul says, "Be careful how you act; these are difficult days. Don't be fools; be wise: make the most of every opportunity you have for doing good. Don't act thoughtlessly, but try to find out and do whatever the Lord wants you to" (Ephesians 5:15–17, TLB).

I think this is powerful advice, don't you? It's exactly the parachute you may need someday when you find yourself in a romantic relationship and the engine fails.

SOMETHING TO THINK ABOUT . . .

- How did you handle your last breakup with the person you were dating?
  - What did you do right?
  - What did you do wrong?
- What did the experience teach you about relationships?
- What will you do differently in your future relationships because of what you've learned?

CHAPTER 9:
SYMBOL OF A LIFETIME, ONE-FLESH COMMITMENT

Tara and Jon are in love. As young adults, they know the difference between infatuation and committed love. Their relationship has weathered some rocky times—and through it all their love continues to grow stronger.

Because both Tara and Jon have plans for graduate study, they realize it may be a few years before they'll be able to marry. But lately they've been feeling some pressure. The hugs are arousing strong responses, and the kisses are becoming more intense. They wonder if waiting until marriage for sex is really necessary or just an old-fashioned concept.

So many of their friends are living together, why shouldn't they? After all, they're totally committed to each other. They're mature, intelligent adults. They know all about safe sex and birth control. And they're planning on being married someday.

Tara and Jon are asking the questions many unmarried couples ask. What's wrong with sex before marriage? Is oral sex outside of marriage permissible? How far can we go before we've crossed the line? How can something be wrong when it makes us feel so good?

I know you've asked these questions. These are legitimate questions, and trite responses aren't going to satisfy. But the answers to these questions won't become clear until you understand why God created sex.

WHY GOD CREATED SEX

For all the really important and wonderful things in God's world, He has given us symbols to help us remember. For example, He made the Sabbath as a reminder of Creation; baptism by immersion, to symbolize burying the sinful body and being raised up to a new life, and the rainbow, to tell us there would never be another worldwide flood. Satan doesn't like God's reminders, and He has done his best to destroy these symbols by creating counterfeits. He's done the same with sex and marriage. Let me explain.

God wants more than anything for us to have a connection with Him. He loves us so much, He promises to live within us and never leave us. But He wants more than a one-way connection. He wants us to respond. He wants an intimate love *relationship* with us.

How can human beings, who live in the physical realm, understand a God who is spiritual? To give us an idea about how close, how satisfying, how electrifying, and how pleasurable this oneness with Him could be, God created sex. It's the highest and most holy physical manifestation of oneness that we can experience. That's why marriage was God's crowning act of creation. For in God's design, sex was never meant to be experienced outside of the lifelong commitment of marriage.

God's desire is for us to enjoy sex at a higher level. Just as man completes a woman and there is a wholeness in joining their bodies, minds, and souls together, God wants to complete us. There should be no shame or guilt as a man and a woman explore the pleasures of sex. It is the closest physical experience that humans can have that can give them a glimpse of what oneness really means.

What better symbol could God design for complete unity than sexual intercourse? Two different individuals, a male and a female, joining together in the highest and most intimate form of human love.

In order for men and women to be constantly reminded of their unity and commitment to each other, God created sexual intercourse to be so exciting, so pleasurable, and so fulfilling that humans would look forward to experiencing it over and over again—each time celebrating and renewing their marital commitment and their commitment to oneness with God.

There is nothing else in the marriage relationship that has this same meaning. Sexual intercourse is the only human act that God reserved exclusively for marriage partners. Each time this oneness is expressed, each time the exciting climax is reached and each body involuntarily responds to the other, it reminds the couple of their lifetime commitment.

That's why adultery is so devastating to a marriage and why it's the only reason God gives for divorce! And that's why Satan is trying so hard to destroy this symbol *before* marriage.

If Satan can counterfeit sexual intercourse so it no longer symbolizes the unity that God intended, then he has diminished the importance of sex within marriage. Instead of sex turning a person's mind to his relationship to a spouse and to God, Satan's plan is to turn a person's mind toward self and the fulfillment of lustful desires without commitment. So far, Satan has been very successful in his quest. In fact, throughout history it is during satanic orgies that the sexual act becomes the most heinous and degrading sin.

There are many ways that Satan has caused sexual intercourse to lose its God-designed meaning of a one-flesh commitment for life. Here are three of the major ones:

1: Sex outside of a marriage commitment. If you have sexual intercourse while dating, it won't hold the same meaning when you are married. In fact, the more people you experience sex with, the less sacred it becomes. Sex is the greatest symbol of a lifetime commitment in marriage. It is important to keep it for your life partner; otherwise it is reduced to merely a pleasurable act or a way to have a baby.

2: Sex with the same gender. If you have "sex" with someone of the same gender—which means oral or anal sex—you destroy its significance. Most homosexual or lesbian relationships aren't stable relationships. Many gays have multiple partners—some can have partners numbering in the thousands. Even with the move toward gay marriages, it is impossible for the sex act between two men or two women to have a one-flesh commitment for life meaning because their anatomy is the same. A man and a woman's body have been designed by God to fit one inside the other to become one flesh. To have sex with the same gender is a counterfeit.

3: Self-stimulated sexual response. Masturbation leading to a sexual climax can diminish the true meaning of sexual intercourse as God designed it. And it could possibly affect a future marriage relationship because it only meets selfish needs.

What follows is more detailed information on premarital sex and masturbation, along with important guidelines to help you make wise sexual decisions. First, consider the risk factors associated with premarital sex.

WHY WAIT?

1: GOD GAVE US GUIDELINES FOR SAFE AND SATISFYING SEX.

God wants the best for us, and because He created sex for our pleasure, He also gave us guidelines so we could experience the joy of this incredible experience without shame and guilt. Here is what God's Word says:

- "Now the body is not for sexual immorality but for the Lord" (1 Corinthians 6:13).
- "Flee sexual immorality . . . he who commits sexual immorality sins against his own body. Or do you not know that your body is the temple of the Holy Spirit who is in you, whom you have from God, and you are not your own?" (1 Corinthians 6:18, 19).
- "This is the will of God, your sanctification: that you should abstain from sexual immorality" (1 Thessalonians 4:3).
- "Fornication and all uncleanness or covetousness, let it not even be named among you, as is fitting for saints" (Ephesians 5:3).

In addition, the book of Proverbs is a helpful guide in the area of sexuality.

2: SEX CAN PUSH COUPLES PREMATURELY INTO MARRIAGE.

Sex can drive a relationship toward marriage, even though the couple has little else going for them. Sex before marriage can cause misunderstandings and false expectations. Often one or both feel guilty, they think they love each other, and because they have already experienced sex, they feel the right thing to do is to get married. In fact, many feel that by having sex they are already married in God's eyes. This isn't true. God wants you to marry the person with whom you will have the best possible chance of becoming everything God wants you to be. So just because you've had sex with someone, it doesn't mean you should marry. Nor is it wise to continue having sex if you want to get married to the person someday. Seldom does friendship grow like it should when a relationship is dominated by sex.

Once you begin to understand the true meaning of sexual intercourse and feel it would be best to wait, you can choose not to have sex again until you're married. Some call this "secondary virginity." Your sexual partner may not understand your decision for abstinence. Some are in a relationship only for sex. If that's the case, it's better to know that as soon as possible. If you decide to continue dating, pray together and ask God to lead you so the pressure to have sex will not be overwhelming. Don't put yourselves into compromising situations. And don't beat yourself up if you've already had sex. We all make choices that have consequences. See this as a learning experience. You don't have to feel guilt and shame. Instead, ask God and your partner for forgiveness and determine with God's help to make wiser decisions in the future.

3: FLASHBACKS OF PREVIOUS SEXUAL ENCOUNTERS CAN HAUNT A MARRIAGE.

You can control your body a lot easier than you can control your mind. People who have participated in premarital sex sometimes complain of flashbacks. "It's like having three people making love in one bed," said one man. "My wife might say something or move in a certain way, and before I know it, my mind is back on the beach somewhere, or in a van having sex with a girl-friend. I'd give anything to get rid of those memories. I really do love my wife, and I want to enjoy our marriage relationship to the fullest."

4: SEX CAN COVER UP SERIOUS DIFFICULTIES IN A RELATIONSHIP.

"The only time we get along is when we're in bed together," one young woman commented. "When we are away from each other, or together and not making out, it's clear we are so different that we should never get married. But once he starts to kiss me and caress my body, it feels so good that I'm convinced we are made for each other."

5: SEX CAN MAKE IT DIFFICULT TO DISTINGUISH BETWEEN REAL LOVE AND INFATUATION.

Infatuation is passionate love—feelings generated by biology, not by reason. While passionate love is a part of true love, it's not the dominating factor.

It is natural for a married couple to seek privacy to enjoy sexual intimacies. This is part of their need to grow together in unity. However, before marriage, one of the major ways to distinguish infatuation from true love is whether the couple is happy only when they are alone with each other. True love draws a couple closer to their families, friends, and God. Infatuation causes a couple to pull away from others. (See chapter 12.)

Because sexual intercourse is designed to bring two people together in the oneness of body, mind, and soul, when it is experienced outside of marriage, it can confuse a person's feelings and decision-making ability. Premarital sex feels like it is enhancing oneness and leads a couple to believe it is safe to go ahead and get married. But the fact is, premarital sex usually promotes only physical unity and not unity of the mind and soul, which is necessary for lifetime commitment. In fact, research studies have generally found that the divorce rate is higher for couples living together before marriage than it is for those who don't.

6: PREMARITAL SEX CAN TRIGGER LIFETIME GUILT AND REGRET.

Premarital sex doesn't have to trigger lifetime guilt, because God forgives. But it can if you let it. You cannot change how you were raised or what has happened to you.

Some have been brought up with strong moral codes and experience shame and guilt when they go against their values and have sex before marriage. Others try to escape guilt feelings by blaming their parents for raising them with high moral standards. Others blame God since these standards are biblical. Then there are those who have hang-ups concerning sexual behavior because of unhealthy patterning or sexual abuse.

Unfortunately, life happens. You can either accept the fact that you've made mistakes or suffered abuse and stay bitter, or you can pursue personal growth because of these experiences. It's your choice. Don't get me wrong. It' a lot of hard work, but if you deal with your sexual issues and give up the baggage before marriage, it will be well worth it. God can give you treasure in the pain or a gem in the fire. So pursue it. What might the treasure or gem be? The opportunity to take your mistakes and the bad things that have happened to you and use them to help others to either make wiser choices or overcome troublesome issues.

If you still have unresolved sexual issues after praying about it and trying on your own, seek a good Christian counselor. God has professionals available to help you work through your hang-ups and dysfunctional feelings so you can have the best possible chance of achieving sexual fulfillment in marriage.

7: GUILT FEELINGS OVER SEX BEFORE MARRIAGE CAN BE CARRIED OVER TO SEX IN MARRIAGE.

If you participate in premarital sex and know it is wrong, it's quite natural to feel guilty. The more times you experience premarital sex, the more times you're likely to feel guilty, until sex becomes associated with guilt. There is a chance that after you marry, having guilt-free sex may be difficult, even though you know it is now OK.

Another method of preprogramming your body is the way some people train their bodies to respond during sexual excitement. Before marriage, knowing that the act of sexual intercourse is wrong, many couples just pet to the plateau stage of sexual arousal and then back away from each other (which, by the way, is very difficult to do). In so doing, they train their bodies to respond only to a certain level and then shut down.

Some individuals who have participated in this practice before marriage find it difficult to achieve the full sexual climax during intercourse because their bodies automatically shut off at a certain point. The next time they have sex with their spouse, they are so worried about not achieving a climax that once again, they don't. What happens sexually is pretty well determined by what goes on in your mind—and how you have trained your body. Once you get married, you can reprogram your body, but it takes time and sometimes professional help.

8: PREMARITAL PREGNANCY.

What are your goals in life? Are you willing to take the chance of having a baby before you are married? What would this do to your ability to get the education you want or the training needed for the career you have always dreamed about.

But pregnancy can be prevented, can't it? Yes and no! The problem is, birth control methods don't always work. If you don't think unintended pregnancy is a problem today, just look at the statistics on abortions and unwed mothers. And the numbers are increasing each year. There is no 100-percent-safe method of birth control, short of sterilization—and even then, accidents do happen.

9: THERE IS AN INCREASED RISK OF CERVICAL CANCER AMONG WOMEN WHO ENGAGE IN SEX WITH MULTIPLE PARTNERS.

That's a fact.

10: AIDS AND OTHER SEXUALLY TRANSMITTED DISEASES.

With most sexually transmitted diseases, such as gonorrhea, syphilis, or genital herpes, you usually know within a few days or weeks whether you have contracted the disease because of obvious physical symptoms. AIDS, however, can stay dormant in your body for up to ten years before you have any symptoms. This means that for ten years a person with AIDS may be unknowingly infecting sexual partners with the AIDS virus. Now that's frightening. Suddenly, staying a virgin—and marrying a virgin—may be a life-or-death matter.

Venereal disease is, in itself, extremely serious if not deadly. And add to this the emotional grief caused by the disease—that alone can ruin a life.

When I mentioned this fact to one of my friends, she told me about a young woman she knew in college who I'll call Cindy. Cindy was a pre-med major, looking forward to a bright future. She had high moral standards and had maintained them for twenty-three years. During her senior year of college she went through a couple of relationships and ended up wondering if she would ever get married. Then Bill came along.

Bill was older, tall, dark, muscular, and handsome—and he drove a racy sports car. Cindy felt truly loved for the first time in her life, but Bill was slow to make a commitment, even though they talked of marriage. On the night he begged her to have sex, she felt this might be the commitment she was looking for. Convinced he really loved her, Cindy said yes, even though all her moral training screamed no.

She gave him her virginity, and he gave her gonorrhea. The stigma of VD (venereal disease) was almost more than Cindy could bear. When she confronted Bill, he claimed he had gotten the disease from her, which only added to her humiliation. Treatments were begun to heal the disease, but nothing could heal her guilt, not even counseling. For a year Bill would have nothing to do with her as he dated and conquered other women. This resulted in her giving up her dream of medical school. Finally, when Bill came back to her, she said Yes to marriage, in spite of the pain he had caused her.

They've been married for almost a year now, but most of Cindy's friends still question Bills' commitment. And Cindy will probably live with the consequences of her decision for life.

11: RESEARCH INDICATES PREMARITAL SEX ISN'T GOOD FOR MARRIAGE.

Even though you can find studies to support anything you want to believe, the vast majority of research indicates that those couples who had sex before marriage are more likely to have their marriages end in divorce, and are more likely to have extramarital affairs. Even though couples who had premarital sex seem to achieve sexual satisfaction sooner after they are married, they are less satisfied overall with their marital sex lives. That's sad, isn't it?

Here's another thing to consider. By having premarital sex—even if a couple later gets married—the woman may be setting her partner up for an extramarital affair. Here's why: when premarital sex is frowned upon by friends, family, church, or a cultural group, experiencing it—with the excitement of possibly getting caught—gives men an adrenaline rush that can be addictive. Once married, because sex is now permissible, they don't feel the same jolt, so they turn to extramarital affairs. Yes, girls, having premarital sex may be training your partner to cheat on you once you're married!

12: IT DESTROYS VIRGINITY.

Virginity is the one gift God has given to each individual to give to his or her marriage partner. Having premarital sex is like handing a million dollars to the wrong person—and you can never get it back for the right one.

But, you might say, "I was raped." Or, "A family member molested me when I was a child." We live in a sex-crazed world where it is estimated that perhaps as many as a quarter to a third of all girls and boys are sexually molested sometime in their young lives. You might be one of these people, and you're thinking your virginity has already been destroyed. But that's not true. You didn't *give* it away—as God designed you should do on your wedding day; *it was stolen*. Sexual abuse can leave you with lurid memories and a distaste for sex, which may require professional counseling to overcome, but because this abuse was not your fault—because you did not choose to be violated—you can enter marriage with the choice of giving yourself fully to your marriage partner. With God nothing is impossible. Accept this gift from God and look forward with eager anticipation to giving it to that special person on your wedding day.

13: IT DESTROYS REPUTATIONS AND RESPECT.

It's almost impossible to keep premarital sex a secret, no matter how hard you try. Eventually someone finds out, or one of the parties feels so guilty that he or she confesses to a third party. What will this knowledge do to your reputation?

Think about it: Do you want to marry someone who has been sexually involved with someone else? Most dedicated Christian young people would rather marry someone who hasn't had sex—at least not someone who they feel has been promiscuous. Having a previous sexual relationship could destroy your chances of dating and marrying the very person who makes your heart sing!

Now turn the tables. Do you have the right to destroy another person's reputation? And what about the respect you have for that person—and for yourself? Do you really want to enjoy sex for a moment only to cause both of you to live with regret for the rest of your lives?

Feelings of self-worth are important. If you do what you know you shouldn't do, you demean your self-respect, which is an important part of your total feelings of personal value. Are a few moments of sexual pleasure worth the loss of your self-respect and someone else's?

14: IT CAN DESTROY TRUST IN A RELATIONSHIP.

Once premarital sex has occurred, there is a very good chance that one or both partners may sometime in the future question, "If this person had sex with me outside the marriage relationship, would he or she do it with someone else?" This can lead to doubt, mistrust, and jealousy in marriage and can destroy it.

15: IT DESTROYS THE VALUE AND MEANING OF THE HONEYMOON.

This reason alone is enough to say No. Of course, it's difficult to understand the significance of a honeymoon when you've never experienced the excitement, the anticipation, and the marvelous sense of fulfillment that is all intended to be a part of your wedding night. Trust me—there is nothing as special as a wedding night. Picture in your mind what you'd like. A beautiful hotel room with roses; maybe a Jacuzzi hot tub just big enough for two; a sexy negligee, perfume, romantic music, and chilled sparkling grape juice—and your beloved. If this romantic atmosphere is where you'd like to give your gift of a lifetime—your virginity—away, why settle for the back seat of a car or a cheap motel room? Every time you're tempted to compromise, picture this scene in your mind. It's worth waiting for.

If you've had sex before marriage, the honeymoon becomes merely a vacation. That's crazy! You will be taking vacations for the rest of your life, but you'll have only one first honeymoon. More than anything else, your honeymoon is a sacred time to discover the love that God intended a man and a woman to experience. This should be your Eden experience—a little bit of heaven on earth.

16. PREMARITAL SEX TENDS TO BE HABIT-FORMING.

This is especially true when sex is experienced with a number of partners. If the sexual act no longer means a one-flesh commitment for life, then there is little to prevent a spouse from finding sexual partners outside the marriage relationship. When sex with various partners has become a habit, and habits become addictions, it's almost impossible for wives or husbands, no matter how good they may be in bed, to be able to continue to satisfy their spouses' increased appetite for novelty and change. It puts the spouse wanting a monogamous relationship in an almost impossible position. If you marry someone who has had multiple sexual partners, you may find your spouse's sexual appetite is very difficult to satisfy.

17: ATTITUDES OFTEN CHANGE AFTER A PREMARITAL SEX EXPERIENCE.

Even though you and your boyfriend or girlfriend think you are madly in love and your love will last a lifetime, premarital sex can do strange things to your feelings. Once you have sex, you will probably experience conflicting emotions, including guilt, that cause you to treat others differently. Your respect for your sexual partner usually decreases. Like dominoes, all your loving feelings begin to tumble, and a reversion reaction can set in. Then, instead of having loving feelings toward this person, you feel resentful, angry, and possibly used.

18: YOU NEVER KNOW WHOM YOU WILL MARRY.

It's not uncommon for a person to date someone for a year or so and then end up marrying that person's sibling, cousin, or best friend. Can you imagine the hurt and the guilt that would result if you have fooled around with one and ended up marrying the other? It happened to Koby. After a few weeks of dating, Koby invited Melissa to move into his apartment, where they enjoyed intimacies that should have been reserved for marriage. Their engagement was announced at a big party at Melissa's parents' house. That's when he met Melissa's younger sister, Maya, for the first time. She had just returned from a year abroad—and he was captivated by her. He loved Melissa and didn't want to hurt her, but the more time he spent with Maya, the more he realized he was engaged to the wrong sister. Maya, however, was loyal to Melissa. She knew Melissa and Koby had been living together, and she refused to give Koby the time of day. He was beside himself. He didn't want to hurt Melissa—but he knew if he married her, his heart would pant for Maya whenever he would see her. Yet, if he married Maya, his memories of sex with Melissa would complicate things. Just thinking about future family reunions made him break out in a cold sweat. He was in a no-win situation. In the end, he lost both.

19. IT DESTROYS THE EXAMPLE YOU WANT TO HAVE YOUR TEENAGERS FOLLOW SOME DAY.

When you're young and experimenting with sex, you seldom think of the future. But twenty years from now when your kids get to those critical teen and early adult years and they ask, "Did you have sex before marriage?" what would you like to be able to tell them? Do you want to have to say, "Do as I say—not as I did." Or would you like to say, "I made a commitment to God and my future mate to keep myself pure, regardless of what my friends were doing or how strongly I was tempted. And I'm glad I did."

But what if you did have sex outside of marriage? All is not lost. Your decisions may not have been God's Plan A for your life, but He can still use you. Plan B might be for you to use this mistake as a ministry tool to help others realize just how important it is to wait for marriage.

20: IT CAN ERODE A RELATIONSHIP WITH GOD.

Sex is God's gift to you to be used under His guidelines. When His guidelines are ignored and you misuse His gift, the guilt feelings may be so strong that if you are not willing to ask forgiveness and change your ways, you may think that the only way you can live without overwhelming guilt is to turn away from God. That is a mistake.

How much better to follow King David's example after he made a series of terrible mistakes. Remember the Bible story? David repented of his sexual sin with Bathsheba and the murder of her husband. He didn't turn bitter against God, even though there were terrible consequences. In the end, God called

David a man after His own heart. What an example to all those who have yielded to the temptation of sex.

Some young people have a negative picture of marriage. Perhaps they have grown up experiencing family violence and abuse. Some have observed their parents' or a friend's marriage to be a state of torment instead of a state of bliss. Others see sex as dirty, as they have observed family members cheating on a spouse. If this has been your experience, you may have developed the attitude that marriage isn't all that great, so why wait?

This is unfortunate. Marriage is truly a beautiful experience and the complete sexual experience is worth saving for your lifetime partner as a gift symbolizing a binding commitment. This is God's plan for your ultimate happiness. But if you've already messed up, God is so good. He can wash you white as snow—and what blessings you will experience if you choose from this day forward, to wait for marriage.

Maybe it's time to sign a commitment to virginity:

Because I believe God has a wonderful plan for my life, which includes experiencing the fullness of physical intimacy with the person I will marry, I pledge to keep my virginity as a gift to give to my mate on our wedding night.

Date: _____ *Signature:* _____

SELF-STIMULATING SEXUAL RESPONSE

Sexual desire reaches its peak for men in the late teens and early twenties and for women in the twenties and early thirties. For many, this intense desire precedes the finding of a spouse and the yearning to settle down into a lifetime marriage relationship. If God created the sexual desire to peak so early, and if sex with someone outside of marriage is wrong, then what about self-stimulation? Masturbation is better than unmarried sex, isn't it?

There has been a lot of discussion about masturbation. Years ago it was taboo. It was believed masturbation caused all kinds of diseases, including blindness and insanity. Today scientists laugh at this. Even some Christian leaders have said that although masturbation isn't necessarily good, it's certainly a lot better than having intercourse with someone else. The problem, they say, is when you entertain lustful thoughts while engaging in self-stimulation. Jesus specifically mentioned lust to be a sin (Matthew 5:27, 28). Lust can lead to pornography, sexual addictions, and feelings of guilt and shame.

Others argue that there is no difference physiologically in the sexual response whether it is from genital penetration or hand-manipulation. Since there is still the excitement phase, the plateau, the climax, and finally the resolution phase, why is sexual intercourse in marriage so good and masturbation so bad?

The answer is that sexual intercourse brings two people committed to each together for life into a closer relationship, while masturbation causes a person to draw away from relationships with others. A study on health habits done by two well-known epidemiologists, Nedra Belloc and Lester Breslow, offers interesting insights.[1] They found that if people kept seven health habits, they lived longer. The health habits were getting adequate sleep, eating breakfast, not eating between meals, keeping a moderate weight, exercising, not smoking, and drinking moderately or not at all.

When two social-epidemiologists, Lisa Berkman and Leonard Syme,[2] got involved, they asked, "If physical health habits are important for longevity, what about social health habits?" They used four questions from the health-habits study that gave an indication of a person's social contacts: (1) Are you married? (2) Do you belong to a church? (3) Are you a member of any social clubs? (4) Do you have close friends and relatives? When they analyzed the data, they found that people who had these four things present in their lives lived longer, regardless of their physical health habits. In other words, we are social creatures, and social contacts are important for health and longevity.

And what does this have to do with masturbation? Sexual intercourse is other-oriented—or should be! Masturbation, however, is merely for self-pleasure. Instead of building relationships, it may actually cause a person to become even more withdrawn. Those who habitually masturbate, sometimes multiple times per day, are often extremely isolated individuals, even though they may be married.

One could apply the chicken and the egg argument to this and ask, "Is it the isolated individual who is drawn to masturbate, or does masturbation cause a person to become isolated?" Regardless, it does appear from research that those individuals who lack a social network and are more isolated don't live as long as others. The implication is that isolated people are less healthy. Could it be that masturbation, per se, may not cause illness, but that isolation does? It's something to consider.

Regardless of these suppositions, masturbation is using the sexual act to do exactly the opposite of what God intended sex to do. Instead of bringing two people closer together, masturbation has a tendency to alienate and isolate. It can also diminish the meaning of a one-flesh marriage commitment for life if lustful fantasies are entertained while a person stimulates him- or herself. And in far too many cases, the person who habitually masturbates is tempted to use pornographic material to heighten the sexual response.

Engaging in sexual fantasies along with masturbation can set up individuals to fulfill their lustful appetites promiscuously. Lust reduces a partner, even a fantasy partner, to merely an object. This results in further isolation (a person-to-object relationship) rather than true intimacy (a person-to-person relationship).

Masturbation can, in some cases, affect an individual's adjustment to marital intercourse. When individuals get into the habit of masturbating, their attention is completely focused on their own arousal, so they soon learn how to bring about a quick and intense response. The objective of sexual intercourse, however, should be to pleasure your partner. Many who masturbate habitually are disappointed in their sexual response during marital intercourse. Because their minds are focused on their partner, their own response may not be as intense as it is when self-stimulated. To find satisfaction, too many of these individuals go back to masturbating rather than drawing close to their spouses and concentrating on learning how to pleasure them. The result? Isolation, alienation and, too often, divorce.

There is nothing wrong in touching your own body and being aware of what stimulates your sexual responsiveness. Good sexual adjustment in marriage is a result of feeling comfortable about your body, knowing what is pleasurable to you, and communicating this to your partner. For many women, a sexual climax is not experienced in the early stages of marriage. In fact, some women go years without having a sexual climax simply because they don't know what stimulation their body needs in order to respond. There is nothing wrong with self-stimulation to learn this information, if the motive is to have a deeper enjoyment of the sexual relationship with a spouse.

But there is no need for extensive experimentation before marriage. In fact, if one chooses to participate in self-stimulation, there may develop an even greater desire for sexual activity, making it very difficult to control sexual urges. God didn't create you to be hot-wired and then have no place to go. If you keep hot-wiring yourself by keeping your mind on sexual things, your body will crave release, and sexual addiction is often the result.

If you're having trouble in this area, take a look at your life. What music are you listening to? What pictures hang on your walls? What movies do you watch? What magazines do you look through? What Internet sites do you visit? Are you eating a healthful diet? Are you getting good exercise? If you answered these questions the way I think you did, then no wonder you're having trouble!

If you keep your mind on serving others and becoming the kind of person God wants you to be, God can help you get through these years of sexual temptation so you can come to marriage with purity and celebrate your union with God's symbol of a one-flesh, lifetime commitment. And here's the additional blessing. As you celebrate oneness with each other, you can have a better understanding of the oneness God wants you to celebrate with Him.

How Far Is Too Far?

There were four questions posed at the beginning of this chapter: What's wrong with sex before marriage? How can something be wrong when it makes us feel so good? Is oral sex outside of marriage permissible? How far can we go before we've crossed the line?

Before reading on, why don't you attempt an answer: _____

_____ .

OK, here's my take on it. Beyond arousal kissing, any actions that might be considered a part of foreplay (which means getting your body ready for a sexual climax) should be reserved for marriage. Why? It's time to read on. I think you'll find more answers in the next chapter.

Something to Think About . . .

- Are you ready to commit your sexual desires to the Lord? Are you ready to trust Him and His plan for their fulfillment? If you've been struggling in this area, I encourage you to go before the Lord and honestly tell Him how you're feeling. Believe me! He won't be shocked at anything you say.
- If someone asked you, "What's wrong with premarital sex?" what would you say?

- If a date pressured you to have sex, what would you do?
- If you knew that a couple who you often double-dated with was having sex, what would you say or do?
  - Do you think it would make any difference in whether you double-dated or not? Explain your answer.
  - Do you feel any different about this couple having learned that they were having sex?

---

1. Nedra B. Belloc and Lester Breslow, "Relationship of Physical Health Status and Health Practices," *Preventive Medicine* (August 1972), 409–421.

2. Lisa Berkman and Leonard Syme, "Social Networks Host Resistance and Mortality: A Nine Year Follow-Up Study of Alameda County Residents," *American Journal of Epidemiology,* vol. 109 (February 1979), 186–204.

CHAPTER 10:
GROWING TOWARD BONDED INTIMACY

We were never meant to be alone. God said it in the beginning, and it's still just as true. We need each other. In fact, we crave intimacy and fear isolation.

Many sexual relationships are entered into because of the mistaken idea that intimacy can be achieved only by having sex. But true intimacy is not physical—it's psychological. It can be psychological and physical, but never just physical. Because sex and intimacy are erroneously equated, too many lonely people jump into bed with strangers and end up dreadfully disillusioned. In their race to what they thought was intimacy, they miss the foundation stages that make true intimacy possible.

Sex, apart from intimacy, is not psychologically satisfying. It may be a release for sexual tension and momentarily exhilarating, but the sex act alone will never fulfill a person's need for true intimacy. Intimacy is achieved when we bare our souls, not our bodies, to each other. It's the sharing of our innermost feelings that breaks the isolation barrier.

When a couple builds their relationship on the foundation of soul sharing and close fellowship, and then pledges their lifelong commitment to each other in marriage, sex is designed to be the crowing act of intimacy. If psychological intimacy has been achieved prior to marriage, then physical intimacy will enhance the commitment. This combination of psychological and physical intimacy is what I call bonded intimacy. This is the ultimate! It's the mountaintop experience every young person dreams of having. It's the warm, cozy feeling that happens when two people psychologically and physically become one. Bonded intimacy can be experienced only within the security of a marriage relationship—and it may not happen on your wedding night. Intimacy grows through experiences of life, creative experimentation, and playful practice!

And you can't rush it. Time is the bonding material. Far too many couples race through the friendship stage of their relationship and head off on their honeymoon without experiencing the psychological oneness that is the necessary foundation for bonded intimacy. They soon become married singles and wonder what went wrong. If you don't want this to happen to you, it is important you don't rush your love relationship. If you do rush and happen to miss a step or two, you will have to backtrack before you can experience the intimacy that God planned for you to find in marriage. So why not do it right the first time?

To help you on your journey toward bonded intimacy, I've created sixteen steps to go through and placed them into four relational stages: friendship dating, serious dating, courtship, and marriage. Take the time to enjoy each step of your journey, won't you? The relationship you build will be worth your efforts.

FRIENDSHIP DATING

The foundation to bonded intimacy is friendship. The friendship stage of a relationship can be experienced with anyone. For couples, however, it's during this stage that casual dating usually occurs. If the steps in this stage are missed or rushed through, a couple will need to regress to this stage in order to achieve a complete sense of intimacy. The four steps within the friendship stage are as follows:

STEP 1: LOOKING WITH INTEREST AT EACH OTHER

There is usually something about a person's appearance, expression, words, or demeanor that draws your attention to that person and makes you want to get acquainted. Every relationship starts out on this level.

Different individuals are attracted by different things. For one it might be the words of a person's prayer. For another it may be the sparkle in someone's eyes, or the way he walks, or the way she smiles. Something will catch your attention and makes you desire a relationship.

If you don't immediately go over and introduce yourself, you begin planning how you can meet. You may talk to others about this person and take note of where he or she hangs out. You might phone or write to suggest a casual date so you can get acquainted. At this point the relationship quickly moves to Step 2.

STEP 2: GETTING ACQUAINTED

This get-acquainted stage is characterized by conversation aimed at finding out about the other person: "Where did you go to school? How many brothers and sisters do you have? What classes are you taking? Where are you working? What church do you attend? What career are you interested in?" At this level ideas and opinions are expressed, and you learn what makes the person unique. Discussions may range from current events to deep theoretical issues. It's during this level that you begin to discover similar interests, and share ideas, passions, and dreams. You also assess whether the person's basic personality is pleasing. The end result, however, is the same—you get to know enough about the person to either walk away from the friendship or move forward. If you like what you're learning, you move on to the next step.

STEP 3: INTIMATE TALKING AND FELLOWSHIP

Step 3 is probably the most important in the bonding process. You now begin to invest large amounts of time into this relationship, and you really get to know each other as you share your dreams, your feelings, and what's on your heart. You develop a deep understanding about where the other is coming from and what makes him or her tick. You empathize with each other. If one hurts, you hurt; if one laughs, you laugh.

During this stage you begin to plan how you can spend more time together, and how you can let the other person know how special he or she is to you. Through words and actions, your message is "I care."

At this point you become vulnerably honest. You bare your soul, revealing to the other who you really are and how you really feel about life. If the feeling is mutual, it brings psychological closeness and satisfaction. If not, this is where a relationship will cease to grow, and you will begin searching for a better match.

The intensity and time commitment required to continue this level of intimacy makes it impossible to have this type of friendship with more than a few people. Girls may have a couple girl friends they can share with at this level, and guys may have a few guy friends. But when it comes to dating, it's at this stage when couples become exclusively interested in each other. Their friends see them as an "item," even though they may not have verbally committed themselves to dating exclusively. It's now that couples begin to desire more meaningful touch, which is the next step within the friendship stage.

STEP 4: MEANINGFUL TOUCHING

Touch is an essential step in achieving intimacy. For some, touch comes easily. I've watched my daughter, for example, cross the college campus and spontaneously hug various people she meets. It's her way of saying "hello," and it has little to do with intimacy. For others touch is difficult, regardless of how close the friendship. It may have to do with the way a person was raised. In some cultures, physical contact—especially between unmarried men and women—is taboo. Others avoid touch because they are afraid they will be rejected. In general, touch—that spontaneous hug or the reaching out for another person's hand—is a natural outgrowth of close, intimate sharing and fellowship.

During Steps 3 and 4 the desire is for a more permanent relationship, which includes more physical contact. If the friendship progresses satisfactorily, the couple will now move from dating around to the more serious dating exclusively stage.

SERIOUS DATING

During this stage, friendship or casual dating, during which the couple is becoming acquainted with each other, takes on a more serious nature. Now there is a desire to date on a steady basis and to become more physically involved. The couple begins to envision what the future might be like with each other. They ask themselves, "How would it be if we were married?" They begin to notice such things as, how this person treats his or her mother or how she reacts under pressure. Is he a family person? Is she good with kids? Does he work well with others? Does she like to cook and manage a home? Are we compatible?

With more physical involvement comes bonding—a *psychological attachment* to each other brought about by touch. Here's a warning: If the physical relationship advances without the *psychological intimacy* which is the result of your growing friendship, you can become physically bonded to another person regardless of your personalities, interests, or cultural differences. As long as a couple experiences physical intimacy through heavy petting or by having sex, the couple "feels" bonded, but they sense something is missing.

Psychological intimacy and psychological attachment are not the same thing. Psychological intimacy is a feeling of oneness. Psychological attachment, caused by physical bonding, leads to dependence, not intimacy. The problem with attachment without intimacy is that you can't go through life constantly holding on to each other. Sooner or later you'll discover that the only thing you have in common is attachment resulting from sex. Unless a couple goes back to Step 3 and begins to build a psychologically intimate friendship, the physical dependence relationship eventually crumbles.

Physical intimacy will come—don't rush it. And it will grow more meaningful and fulfilling, especially when it is built on psychological intimacy, not attach-ment. So don't advance through these next stages unless your friendship has been well established and you have determined that this person has good mar-riage potential. In other words, you have many things in common, the person has most of the qualities that you are looking for in a mate, your personalities are compatible, and you have become best friends.

There is a trend in some Christian circles to bring back the old idea of court-ship, in which the fellow talks with the girl's parents to ask permission to "court" their daughter with the intent of marrying her. If parents aren't available, the guy might ask the girl for her permission. What are the merits of this type of courtship? The fellow's intentions concerning dating are clear—he is interested in marriage. No commitment is made when asking permission, but it does gain the good will of parents early in the relationship, and everyone is clear where the relationship is heading when the couple begins seriously dating.

In contrast to this idea of courtship, many young people today proceed to serious dating without seriously considering marriage. In fact, some couples aren't even interested in marriage—especially when sex is a part of their dating relationship. Some don't even talk about marriage until a proposal is made. Most couples, however, fall somewhere in between these two extremes.

Regardless of what type of courtship you prefer, here are the important steps toward bonded intimacy that occur within the serious dating stage.

STEP 5: DESIRING PHYSICAL TOUCH

The desire to hold hands, kiss, and embrace may have been present from the moment of attraction, but now this desire is no longer inhibited. As a result, the next few steps happen rather quickly.

STEP 6: SIDE-BY-SIDE HAND HOLDING SYMBOLIZING TOGETHERNESS

Now the couple has a desire to let the world know about their special friend-ship. They want to be seen as a couple. Holding hands in public symbolizes their relationship.

STEP 7: TOUCH THAT DRAWS A COUPLE TOGETHER

When the arm is placed around the shoulder or the waist, it symbolizes the couple being drawn together in a special way. Usually an arm around the shoulder comes first. Moving the hand down the body to waist-level symbolizes a more intimate relationship.

STEP 8: FRIENDSHIP KISSING

Although a friendship kiss may have been placed on the hand, cheek, or lips of a friend during the friendship stage, kissing now becomes more frequent and more intense. Once kissing becomes an expected part of a relationship, a couple enters a danger zone. Why? Because mouth-to-mouth kissing is sexually arousing and can quickly lead to other touching behavior that prepares the body for intercourse.

There is nothing wrong with a simple goodnight kiss, but when a couple engages in French kissing with open mouths and probing tongues, their bodies become excited, and there is a desire for sexual release. This desire can move a dating relationship toward marriage before the couple is psychologically prepared for a lifelong commitment.

COURTSHIP

Courtship is the transition stage between dating and marriage. You have made the decision that the person you're dating is a suitable marriage partner. With this realization, the desire for physical intimacy is increased. That's why it's good to have a long friendship stage and a short engagement. It is usually during this stage that the proposal and engagement happens.

STEP 9: AROUSAL KISSING

Arousal kissing is like an explosive bombshell in a dating relationship. Once this bombshell goes off, it is very hard, if not impossible, to backtrack physically. When awakened to the intense feelings of passion, your body desires more. That's the way God designed a man and a woman. Without control in this area, a relationship can quickly—sometimes too quickly—be swept through the other courtship stages.

STEP 10: PLEASURING EACH OTHER WITH TOUCH TO NONSEXUAL AREAS

Nonsexual touch such as rubbing someone's back, gently stroking the arms, legs, or head, and tracing the lips or nose with your fingers becomes a natural part of the relationship. You feel comfortable touching each other. This type of touching is not always initiated with the motive to sexually arouse the other. It is merely an expression of deep desire and caring. It is satisfying just to know that someone has accepted you so completely that touch can be experienced without hesitation. Being comfortable with touch is an important step toward bonded intimacy.

STEP 11: EXTENDED EMBRACING

Passion intensifies at this point when words of love usually accompany extended holding, kissing, and stroking (sometimes called petting). Now you feel comfortable just being in someone else's arms, and you yearn to be held for long periods of time. At last you feel like you belong to someone.

STEP 12: TALKING ABOUT SEXUAL EXPECTATIONS WITHIN MARRIAGE

Be careful how you talk or the language you use during courtship because it can move your relationship forward more quickly than you may realize. Talking about sexually explicit acts, making comments about your own or your partner's sexual arousal, and discussing what turns you on is private talk. It's like psychologically undressing in front of someone. *And it has a bonding effect.*

These things should be shared before marriage, but be careful not to share them too soon. Why? Because once certain things have been said, you will never again be truly private. When you exchange sexual word pictures, you have advanced to a new level of intimacy. Before going there, ask yourself, "Is this where I want to be in this relationship?"

Sexually explicit talk should be reserved for the last few months before marriage, since the next step toward bonded intimacy is to experience physically what you have expressed in words.

MARRIAGE

Sexual stimulation beyond arousal kissing and stroking of nonsexual body parts should be reserved for marriage. If you limit your physical involvement in this way, the next four steps toward bonded intimacy will be celebrated on your wedding night and ideally be continued throughout the years of your marriage. Sex is an amazing act in which couples bring together body, mind, and soul as their intimacy deepens into oneness.

Enjoy the first twelve steps of the bonding process to the fullest during the months of your courtship, and leave the last four to celebrate within the context of a committed lifetime love relationship. If you do, you will experience the intimacy that God designed you to have within marriage. If you don't, the chances are greater that you'll experience sex without intimacy and be deeply disappointed.

Because this book isn't a marriage manual, the last four steps toward bonded intimacy are only listed. These will occur in rather rapid succession as you discover each other within the bonds of marriage.

STEP 13: AROUSAL KISSING PLUS TOUCHING CLOTHED BODY PARTS, INCLUDING BREASTS, BUTTOCKS, AND GENITALS

STEP 14: FOREPLAY

STEP 15: GENITAL STIMULATION

STEP 16: INTERCOURSE

ONCE BONDED, NOT ALWAYS BONDED

Like epoxy glue, many people feel that once you're bonded, you're always bonded. But that is not so. Human relationships need regular re-bonding experiences to maintain intimacy—even within marriage. Each day should be started with Step 1 of the bonded intimacy process as you notice things about the other which you find attractive—things that make you want to renew your relationship. You and your partner are constantly growing and changing. Each day you are a slightly different person from the one you were the day before. That's why you need to spend time getting acquainted with each other as you did in Step 2, sharing your ideas and opinions. If you don't, it may not be long before you're living with a stranger.

The problem with most marriages, and why very few couples experience the intimacy they thought they would find within marriage, is that they skip Step 3 (the sharing of feelings and fellowship) and move right on to Step 4 (a friendship hug or meaningful touch). They then advance quickly through arousal kissing and the rest of the sixteen steps, thinking that the sexual experience is all they need to keep their marriage intact. But there is no shortcut. Without investing the time it takes to share daily with one another what's on your heart and grow together, you may have fleeting moments of oneness, but true intimacy—bonded intimacy—will never be yours.

BONDING AND BREAKUP

Bonds can be broken. A breakup can occur anywhere along this process of growth. The important thing to remember is that while it takes time to become bonded, it also takes time to become unbonded. The farther along in the process you are when a breakup occurs, the more painful the breakup will be and the longer it will take to become free from the bonds you have established.

I have known men and women who knew that if they married a certain person it would spell disaster, yet they allowed themselves to move so far up the steps to bonded intimacy that breaking up was almost impossible. When breakups do happen at this advanced stage, memories take time to fade. Weeks, months, and sometimes years later, you might dream about the person and suffer feelings of loss and regret.

If you think your feelings of loss will automatically go away if you become intimately involved in another relationship, you are mistaken. It is possible to be double bonded. It is possible to be in love with two people at the same time. This is an agonizing situation to find yourself in. It's not fair to you or those you're bonded to.

Do yourself a favor: bury the old before getting seriously involved with the new. Sometimes that means getting rid of the items that carry memories of the other person. Maybe you hung around with certain people, and seeing them brings back memories. You may need to work on making new friendships to give yourself time to heal. Sometimes you need a complete change in environment because everything you see reminds you of your old love.

Kyla was double bonded. After dating Mark for five years, she knew he would never treat her with the respect she wanted, so she broke up. Soon after, she fell in love with a man who had all the qualities she was looking for, but she couldn't forget Mark. Depression followed. She thought she was going crazy.

A good physical examination revealed some nutritional imbalances in her system that were corrected. And through the help of a counselor she decided to attend a college across the country to distance herself from things that reminded her of her first love. Good health, time, and distance healed the double bonding.

If you're having trouble giving up a past relationship, talk things through with a trained counselor. With professional help, you can sort out your feelings and put away the past, so you can be free to move into the future.

THE BONDING POWER OF FIRST LOVE

Many individuals who have broken up after experiencing the intense closeness of the bonding experience find themselves questioning love the second time around. Though they have an intimate friendship relationship, for some reason the intense feelings of the first-love experience are just not there. They question, "Is this true love?"

If you find yourself asking this question, remember that the intensity of feeling you experienced the first time around is not a true barometer to measure the type of love that will make it through a lifetime. You are a different person now. Older and wiser. You see things more maturely. The strength of bonded intimacy is not the fickleness of feeling; it is much deeper, more meaningful, and more satisfying. If the relationship is psychologically intimate, feelings will follow.

Bonding does not happen suddenly. Bonding is a process—a series of steps that two people go through as they become more psychologically and physically involved with each other. The end result is a growing sense of intimacy that has the potential of becoming bonded intimacy in marriage. This is the icing on the cake experience that couples dream about but few take the time to create.

Make bonded intimacy your goal—and enjoy each step of your journey along the way.

SOMETHING TO THINK ABOUT . . .

- Evaluate your present relationship (or a previous one if you're not currently involved with someone).
  - ○ Have you skipped any of the steps to bonded intimacy?
  - ○ What can you do to backtrack and work on that area of your relationship?
- List three things you can do in the next few months to specifically fulfill the purpose of the step (or steps) you feel should be enhanced.

CHAPTER 11:
COURTSHIP COMMUNICATION

"Now that it's all over," said one old-timer to another, "which do you think was worse, the Great Depression, or Bush's bailout of the banks?"

"Well," replied his friend, "I'm a pretty optimistic person, myself, so I don't know much about depression. But I am definitely against bailing out banks and bushes. It just causes too much erosion."

We laugh at the obvious misunderstanding. But the sad fact is that a lack of communication is no laughing matter, especially when it comes to marriage.

I once asked a pastor who did a lot of counseling what he considered to be the three most important things couples could do to keep their marriages vibrant and alive. He responded, "Number 1: Talk. Number 2: Talk. And Number 3: Talk!" Marital success depends on keeping the channels of communication open.

It doesn't take long for a lack of communication to destroy a marriage. That's why it's important to learn the principles of good communication during your courtship. Now is the time to listen for the feelings behind the words, tune into body language, and learn how to say what's on your mind so it sounds to the other person "like apples of gold / In settings of silver" (Proverbs 25:11), and not like "continual dripping on a very rainy day" (Proverbs 27:15). (You'll have to look up those Bible texts to understand the full significance!)

Most of us talk without evaluating our words first. We say exactly what's on our minds, and that's what gets us into trouble. But with a little thought and some training, we can smooth out the rough edges of what we say, getting our messages across without causing hard feelings or misunderstandings.

There's no better time to learn these skills than now, during the dating and courtship period of your life. What follows are some of the most important principles of effective communication. If you faithfully follow these guidelines, ideally by the time you say, "I do," these patterns will have become habitual, and the potential for conflict between the two of you will be significantly reduced.

PRINCIPLE 1: NEVER SAY ANYTHING YOU WOULDN'T WANT SOMEONE TO SAY TO YOU.

It may need to be said, but think first about how would you want this message delivered to you. Cushion your communication with respect and the kindest language possible. In addition to choosing your words carefully, think about what you're communicating with the tone of your voice, your body language, and your attitude. Does it put the other person on edge, make him feel bad, or crush her spirit? And remember, there is a right time and a wrong time to say something. Don't lash out in the heat of a moment. Instead, wait for tempers to cool. Applying the golden rule, to treat others as you want to be treated, will save you much grief—and a lot of apologies.

PRINCIPLE 2: SHARE YOUR FEELINGS BEFORE YOU ARE FORCED TO ACT THEM OUT.

God gave you emotions. Positive feelings guide you toward the person God created you to be. Negative ones warn you that this is *not* who you are, or it is *not* what you like.

Emotions aren't necessary good or bad—it's what you do with them that count. Some think that rather than risk an argument, a person should bury negative emotions and try to forget them. But buried feelings don't die. Instead, they grow in the dark places of your heart until they end up causing ulcers or explosions—neither of which is very good for your health or your relationship.

Here's what to do: learn to recognize a negative feeling when it first appears and do something to get rid of it while it's still small and manageable. If you do, you won't have to act it out later when it's big and ugly and can no longer be contained. When you lose control and act out negative feelings, such as anger or jealousy, it's quite likely that you will do or say something that will end up hurting someone. And the problem only gets worse, not better.

Let's say it's our anniversary. I come home early to fix a special meal. I even pick flowers for a centerpiece. My husband comes into the kitchen holding the newspaper, gives me a quick kiss, sits down at his place, comments, "Smells great!" then opens the paper and begins reading.

I'm hurt. He hasn't noticed the flowers—nor does he mention our anniversary. I expected a gift and some extra attention, but receive neither. After serving the food, I sit down and try to talk, but it's difficult over the newspaper, so I finally give up, and go silent. All the time, my anger is growing. After a few minutes, I'm so furious at him that I don't even feel like eating. I get up, put my dish in the dishwasher and walk out of the room.

He calls, "Honey, what would you like to do tonight?"

"Nothing," I say in a hollow tone.

"Nothing?" he questions. "But it's our anniversary. I thought we could take a moonlight walk in the park—and I have something special for you."

"I'm tired!" I reply without thinking. All I want to do now is get back at him. I'm thinking, *After the way he treated me, he doesn't deserve any of my attention!* So, I put on my old pajamas and get into bed—as far over on my side as I can. And when I hear him coming up the stairs, I pretend I'm asleep.

Isn't that a crazy way to act? My small, almost insignificant hurt feelings turned into negative actions that will not only hurt my husband but probably make him angry. And that's when either the sparks fly—or the silent treatment becomes abusive.

There is a better way to deal with negative feelings. Let's go back and put a different ending to the story. When my husband comes through the door with a quick kiss, no appreciation of the preparation I've done, and begins reading the newspaper, I'm tempted to feel hurt. At this point I have a choice. I can either go into a downward spiral that will hurt both of us, or I can be aware of what I want, take charge, and change history.

When he gives me a quick kiss, I can try to seduce him into a long passionate one. It's fun! And when I think he's forgotten our anniversary, I can say, "I just want to thank you for seven amazing years of my life. Happy Anniversary, sweetheart." When he doesn't recognize the flowers, I mention, "Sweets, look at those pretty flowers, aren't they beautiful?" And to get rid of the newspaper, I can gently and respectfully suggest, "Because it's our anniversary, could you put the paper down while we eat. When I do the dishes you can catch up on things." And if I think he has forgotten a gift, "That's OK. You're the best gift ever!"

How do you think he'll respond? He'll probably take me in his arms, and after our special meal, we'll take a moonlight walk in the park and . . . well, you get the picture.

Do you think he'll forget our anniversary next year? I doubt it! In a non-threatening way, I've communicated what's important to me, and he'll likely get the message.

The key to controlling negative feelings so they don't damage a relationship is to immediately do something to get rid of them before they get out of hand.

PRINCIPLE 3: LISTEN TO THE OTHER PERSON'S FEELINGS.

Feelings can be expressed in words as well as body language, so we must learn to pay attention to both. It has been estimated that only 10 percent of what we actually communicate comes from our words, while 25 percent is from the tone of our voice, and 65 percent comes from nonverbal body language. Because nonverbal communication is so important, we must learn to listen to more than words.

Look beyond the words when you are confronted with something that sounds a little critical. Our tendency is to get so wrapped up in trying to defend ourselves that we miss the underlying issue.

However, if you perceive a negative emotion in what's being said, allow the person to talk about it. Look interested and say something like, "I know you are angry about what I just did; I can tell by the way you are looking at me." Then be quiet and give the other person a chance to voice what's on his or her heart.

When your partner experiences negative feelings, search for the cause. By doing so you can learn about his or her likes or dislikes to help you avoid similar conflicts in the future.

If any advice could top the counsel to talk, talk, talk, it would be to look past the words to try to figure out the underlying issues, and listen, listen, listen. If you follow this wisdom when you or your partner is experiencing negative emotions, you'll find these feelings will be defused and will probably go away.

PRINCIPLE 4: AVOID DOOR SLAMMERS THAT CUT OFF
COMMUNICATION.

A door slammer is what is usually said right before someone screams, "Why can't you understand me!" These are words or phrases that inhibit conversation rather than encourage it. Door slammers hurt people's feelings and make them want to retreat rather than stick around and listen to more. Here are a few of the most popular door slammers:

Commanding: "I thought I told you to return those books to the library."

Threatening: "If you can't remember to return the books on time, you're just going to have to pay the fine."

Moralizing: "If you would just do what you were supposed to do, life would be much more pleasant."

Giving advice: "Next time write down what you were supposed to do so you won't forget."

Arguing: "Don't try to give me some lame excuse. The simple fact is that you forgot."

Criticizing: "You're always forgetting to do what you are supposed to do. Why can't you use your head for what it's meant to be used for?"

Ridiculing: "If you tied a string around your finger, you'd probably forget what it was there for."

Analyzing: "One of the reasons you are so forgetful is probably because you have so much on your mind and don't listen to me when I'm trying to tell you something."

Questioning: "You forgot to return the books! Why did you do that?"

Withdrawing: "I don't want to hear about it. It's your problem, not mine."

Sympathizing: "Oh, you poor baby. You must feel terrible about forgetting those books."

Patronizing: "You're such a perfect person. You're always so reliable and trustworthy. That's why I'm surprised you forgot."

Just think about how you'd feel if these things were said to you. Would it make you want to continue a conversation? I doubt it. Chances are, after too many of these comments, you'd throw up your hands in frustration, run from the room, and slam the door!

PRINCIPLE 5: USE DOOR SOPENERS FOR BETTER UNDERSTANDING.

Instead of the door-slammer approach, why not try these five door-opener techniques? These are nice warm fuzzy messages to encourage continued sharing.

The first door opener is *body language*. Show that you are listening by looking at the other person's eyes, leaning forward, and using a facial expression of interest.

Second, use *acknowledgments* such as, "Yes," "Oh," "That's interesting," "Hmmm," and other audible comments to show you are interested and listening.

Third, *silence*. Yes, silence can be positive, especially when used with interested body language and a few acknowledgments that show you care. Silence can give the space a person needs to think about what to say next. When you are silent and using positive body language, you are nonverbally saying, "I want to hear what is happening to you, and I'm going to be quiet long enough to hear it." Or, "I accept your feelings, whatever they are. I'm not here to change you." Or, "I trust you to decide what you want to say to me. You are in charge of those decisions right now."

Silence is effective only when your body language says, "I'm listening." When silence is used too often or for too long of a time, it's counterproductive.

Fourth, offer *invitations* for the person to say more, like: "Would it help to talk about it?" "It's hard to talk about some things." "Tell me in your own way." "How is it going for you?" "That's interesting." Or, "Anything else?"

Fifth, *reflecting* or *restating* what the person has said in slightly different words is a great way to open the door to more conversation and defuse negative emotions. Reflection lets the other person know you are listening and checks your understanding of what he or she means. For example, if someone explodes, "I've had it with my boss. He told me off in front of the entire staff, and the problem wasn't my fault. When we finally made him realize his mistake, he didn't even apologize!" A reflective response to defuse the anger might be, "Being told off when it's not even your fault is maddening." "It hurt you when he spoke so harshly," or "You weren't prepared for his tirade," or "It's no fun to be verbally abused, especially in front of others." Do you get the idea? A reflection is a nonjudgmental statement that gives the other person permission to continue talking and defuses negative emotion.

PRINCIPLE 6: NEVER WALK AWAY FROM AN ARGUMENT AND POUT.

There is nothing that makes a person feel more rejected than to have a loved one go silent, especially when you're in the middle of a conflict that desperately needs to be resolved.

Giving someone the silent treatment—or pouting—is childish. Everyone gets his or her feelings hurt occasionally, but the mature thing to do is to face the problem and solve it. The worst thing you can do is retreat. The silent treatment often results in isolation. Married couples who use the silent treatment quickly discover that there is nothing quite as big as a bed with two pouting people in it! Believe it or not, some strong-willed couples have lived with "polite" silence for years, each so angry at the other that they would rather starve to death than break down and say, "Please, pass the potatoes."

Of course, you don't want this to happen to your relationship. But the chances are quite high that there will be times ahead when you will feel so frustrated with each other that you'll have to resist the natural urge to pout or walk away in silence.

There is a way to deal with those situations. Put the reason for your "walking away" behavior into written words. Next time you're ready to give the silent treatment, try saying, "You are not listening to me, and I feel like clamming up or walking away and slamming the door. When I talk with you, I sometimes feel I don't get a fair chance to express myself. It's important to me that you understand where I'm coming from. I don't want to talk about it anymore right now because I'm having trouble communicating my feelings. Instead, I'd like to take a half hour or so to write down how I'm feeling. Then I'd like you to read it and we can discuss it. But promise me you won't be defensive or critical. Just listen to what I have to say, and let's try to solve this problem. If we still have trouble communicating, I'd like you to write your response to me."

Writing down an argument may seem like a waste of time, but it does a number of important things. First, when you are forced to write down how you feel, you begin to clarify your thinking, and often the result is that your written words will make more sense than what you say off the top of your head.

Second, writing your responses gives both of you time to think about what the other has said without being influenced by a tone of voice or body language. You can read and reread the message. Many times this reflection period allows tense, hostile feelings to mellow, and your responses to each other are more civil and much more conducive to solving the problem.

To cushion your written response and make it as pleasant as possible, here are a few helpful techniques. Start your written message with a prayer for your partner, and then add a sincere compliment. This cushions the tough stuff which is the heart of your message. To soften your close you might want to add another prayer or an honest word of appreciation. You'll be surprised how effective this method is for solving conflicts. But you'll never really know until you try.

PRINCIPLE 7: CONFRONT EACH OTHER WITH I-MESSAGES, NOT YOU-MESSAGES.

An I-message allows you to take the responsibility for what has happened. A You-message blames the other person. Note the difference: "I get frustrated when I find newspapers and dirty clothes all over the place," versus, "You are so messy. Why can't you put the newspapers where they belong and toss your dirty clothes in the hamper?"

It's not easy to keep the *you* out of a message when you are convinced that if the other person would just shape up, everything would be fine. But the safest way to confront someone with something you don't like is to keep the *you* completely out of the message. This takes practice. To get you started, change the following You-messages into statements that avoid the *you* completely. If you get stumped, you'll find possible answers at the end of the chapter. But don't peak at my answers until you've tried to come up with your own.

1. "I don't like it when you use my things without asking."
2. "I'm tired of listening to you gripe about my parents."
3. "I feel jealous when you spend so much time with other people."

PRINCIPLE 8: DON'T TRY TO SOLVE PROBLEMS WHEN YOU'RE ANGRY.

It's important to listen to each other's feelings and defuse or diminish them before problem solving. When most couples become angry with each other, they make the mistake of trying to solve the problem immediately. The result is usually a shouting match that ends up with both opponents hurling verbal weapons at each other. That's no way to solve a problem. Verbal conflict only causes emotional wounds—and may even lead to physical abuse.

When you both are eager for a resolution to your conflict but you are upset, you should carefully and prayerfully go through the following problem-solving steps.

First, *clarify the problem.* What is it that you disagree about? Be as specific as possible. There may be a number of issues involved, but it's best to deal with one at a time.

Second, *begin brainstorming about possible solutions.* Don't try to evaluate your ideas during this stage, or you may reject a crazy idea that could turn out to be a creative solution. Accept every suggestion, no matter how off-the-wall it may seem. When you have exhausted all the possibilities, you can move on to the next step.

Third, *evaluate your brainstorming ideas,* discarding those that are unacceptable to either of you. As you attempt to find a solution, look for ways to compromise by combining two possible solutions or making slight changes in one idea so it becomes acceptable to both of you. The key to success at this point is to be willing to compromise.

Fourth, *choose the best solution and determine when it will be put into effect.* If you can, pick a specific date.

Fifth, *indicate in some way that you both accept this solution.* Kiss, bring out the cherry cheesecake and celebrate, or sign on the dotted line.

Sixth, *continue to evaluate the situation* to make sure the solution is working. If it isn't working, you've got to go back to the bargaining table and begin brainstorming and compromising again.

There is no problem so difficult that two people willing to compromise can't solve. The key is that both people in a relationship must be willing to compromise. Solutions are rare when one person consistently must give in to the other in order for problems to be solved.

PRINCIPLE 9: AGREE ON SOME BASIC RULES FOR COMMUNICATING FEELINGS.

Here are some rules you might want to establish early on in your relationship. They'll help you keep your discussions about feelings "fair" so you can avoid conflict during those vulnerable moments.

Rule 1: Feelings are neither good nor bad; they just exist. If you feel them, regardless of whether they are reasonable or not, *they are real* and must be listened to and healed with understanding.

Rule 2: Each person owns his or her own feelings. In other words, you choose whether to let something bother you, whether it's what someone says or does. An expression of a negative feeling should not be interpreted as personal criticism. Here's an example. When your boyfriend says, "I feel angry when you're not on time," you could take it to mean, "It's all your fault. If you were on time, I wouldn't be angry." This will probably cause you to become defensive, resulting in an argument. Or you can realize that being on time is important to your boyfriend and try to figure out how you can be on time.

Agree that you will be responsible for your own reactions. A person doesn't make you angry—you choose to allow a certain situation to make you angry. When you own your feelings, you're able to discuss these feelings without the fear that you will hurt the other person's ego or cause him or her to become defensive. Talking about emotions helps to defuse them.

Don't resent it when someone mentions a negative feeling. Instead, use the door-opener techniques to encourage the person with the feeling to talk about it. Maybe you could respond, "It embarrasses you when I make you late for an appointment." When the emotion has been defused, you can add, "How should we solve the problem?"

Rule 3: Don't bring up controversial topics unless you both have the time and energy to finish the conversation. Sometimes you may need to put hot topics on the back burner until you both are ready to deal with them. But be up front and say, "I want to discuss the way I feel when we go to parties together, but now is not a good time. When do you think you would have time to sit down and spend some time resolving this issue?" Or you might simply say, "I need to talk with you about a few things. It's not urgent, but I think it might take a while. When is a good time for you?"

Rule 4: If something is bothering you, don't bury it. Promise each other you will not walk away from an issue that needs to be talked about and solved. If you can't do it immediately, make an appointment.

Rule 5: If either one of you feels unsatisfied with the way you're communicating, agree that you will go to a counselor. You may not feel the need for a counselor, but if the other person does, that is reason enough to go and seek help. If followed, this rule would help lower the divorce rate.

PRINCIPLE 10: AVOID HABITS OF SPEECH THAT ANNOY OTHERS.

Annoying habits of speech get in the way of effective communication. Here are a dozen of the most offensive.

Habit 1: Not looking at the other person when you are talking to them. Eye-to-eye contact is important.

Habit 2: Using big, impressive words. For example, *gargantuan* instead of *huge*.

Habit 3: Repeating yourself. Say something once and move on—don't say it over and over to try to get your point across.

Habit 4: Excessive agreement. Always agreeing, no matter what someone else says, gets obnoxious.

Habit 5: Excessive disagreement. It's also obnoxious when someone constantly takes the antagonist position.

Habit 6: Talking too much. No one likes to be around someone who has to comment about everything. It's especially offensive when the person is always talking about himself.

Habit 7: Quibbling over minutia. Some things are so insignificant that it's not worth arguing about. It's really annoying when someone is constantly picking an argument over something that really doesn't matter.

Habit 8: Under-responsiveness. Have you ever tried to have a conversation with someone who hardly ever responds?

"Wasn't that a super game?"

"It was OK."

"What did you think about that ninth inning double that tied the score?"

"OK."

"And that pitcher was something else!"

"Yah."

Do you get the idea? No one wants to get stuck on a date with an under-responder, much less marry one.

Habit 9: Making over generalizations. "She's always talking." "He never dresses right." "You always get the last word." Seldom is something "always" or "never." Be specific. If you like something that someone does, say, "Hey, that was a neat piano solo," rather than, "You always play perfectly." "You wore that yellow tie last week," is more acceptable than, "You always wear the same thing."

Habit 10: Making illogical comments. It's really aggravating when you are deep in a conversation and someone says something that's way out in left field—completely irrelevant. Keep on the subject, and your contribution to a conversation will be a lot more meaningful.

Habit 11: Making assumptions without adequate information. Let's say you've said something like, "The party wasn't what I expected." It's just a simple statement of fact. The last thing you need is somebody making an assumption like, "Well, I know why you didn't enjoy it. Bonnie wasn't there. You two just can't get along without each other."

Habit 12: Expressing put-downs and pessimism. No one likes a habitual pessimist who can't find anything good to say about anybody or anything. It's unsafe to be around someone who is always critical because chances are you'll be criticized next. Lift people up, don't put them down, and you'll be a much more desirable conversationalist.

WHAT IS GOOD COMMUNICATION?

Good communication is a dialogue, not a monologue. Listen to what Elizabeth O'Connor, in her book *Cry Pain, Cry Hope* has to say about this:

Dialogue is more than your giving me space to say my words, and my giving you space to say yours. It involves our listening. We are all different. We cannot have dialogue unless we honor the differences. How can I build a bridge across the gulf between me and you unless I am aware of the gulf? How can I communicate with you unless I see how things look from your side?

Dialogue demands that I leave the place where I dwell—the landscape of feelings and thoughts that are important to me—in order to dwell for a time with your thoughts, feelings, perceptions, fears, hopes. I must deny myself—forsake the familiar, give up my life—in order to experience your life.

The purpose of dialogue is never to persuade another person to accept our opinions, or values, or view of the world; rather it is to create understanding—a climate where communion takes place. He who has lost himself finds himself. The deepest craving of every heart is to be laid bare, to be known, to be understood. . . .

But how many of us can take time to understand, or even time to make ourselves understood? There is always some place to go, or something to do, secrets to protect.

And if we do not take time to understand each other, how can we take time to understand God?[1]

Ideas to think about, aren't they?

Communication is what keeps a relationship alive. Don't let a day slip by without it. In fact, you would be wise to plan talk time into your schedule. Maybe you would enjoy taking a long walk together each evening or turning off the television while you eat so you can talk without interruption. This planned communication time will become even more important after marriage where you'll find there is the tendency to get wrapped up in your own personal schedule or distracted by children.

Start practicing the principles of good communication during your courtship. Don't get married without it.

SOMETHING TO THINK ABOUT . . .

- Think of the communication you have not only with the person you're dating, but also with your friends, your family, and your coworkers.
  - When does communication break down?
  - What can you do to improve communication between you and those you come in contact with?
- Pick one of the principles mentioned in this chapter and consciously work at incorporating it into your life.

POSSIBLE ANSWERS TO YOU-MESSAGES / I-MESSAGES

I don't like it when my things get used without my permission.

I'm tired of hearing my parents criticized. Or, It makes me angry when my parents are criticized.

I feel jealous when other people seem to get more of your attention than I do.

---

1. Elizabeth O'Connor, *Cry Pain, Cry Hope* (Waco, Tex: Word, Inc., 1987), 39, 40.

CHAPTER 12:
DISCOVERING THE DIFFERENCE BETWEEN ROMANTIC ILLUSIONS AND TRUE LOVE

You've heard the warning "Love is blind," usually spoken by someone shaking her head. That saying is only partly true. True love sees clearly and realistically, even if only partially. It is romantic love—infatuation—that is blind.

Beware of the powerful force of romantic love.

Romantic love is merely an illusion that fades all too quickly. True love has the beautiful blend of passion and accountability, spontaneity and design, tenderness and strength, innocence and reason. This is the kind of love that can last a lifetime.

Romantic love is short lived and one-dimensional. It's a totally absorbing type of love, binding two people in a whirlwind of bliss that makes them oblivious to reason and reality. Romantic love is blind!

Romantic love can grow into lifetime love if a couple has no hidden pathology from their pasts, and if their personalities are compatible, their interests are similar, and their commitment to each other is based on more than feelings. But you can never assume that this intense short-term love will simmer into a lifelong love affair.

Because marriage shouldn't take place during the passionate stage of a romance, how can you tell what type of love you are experiencing? You'll find the answer by carefully considering your responses to the following questions. If you're currently seriously dating, it might be helpful to ask your parents or close friends how they see your relationship.

1: HAS YOUR LOVER SWEPT YOU OFF YOUR FEET IN A WHIRLWIND ROMANCE THAT HAS TAKEN YOUR BREATH AWAY AND LEFT YOU WEAK-KNEED?

If yes, be careful. True love doesn't happen suddenly. Regardless of what you may have heard, no one really falls in love at first sight. You may be attracted to each other and feel an immediate emotional high. You may have sensed, from the moment your eyes met, that you were right for each other. You may feel in love, but true love—love that will last a lifetime—takes time to develop and grow. Don't rush a good thing. Savor every day of love as a gift from God. And if it is meant to be, it will pass the test of time.

2: ARE YOU MORE IN LOVE WHEN YOU ARE TOGETHER THAN WHEN YOU ARE BY YOURSELF? OR ARE YOU IN LOVE WITH THE WRITER OF LOVE LETTERS AND FIND YOURSELF CONFUSED WHEN YOU ARE TOGETHER?

Love does not fluctuate according to the presence or absence of the one you love. Do you love a person more when you are together? If so, it may be that your judgment is being influenced by the charm and excitement of his or her presence. When your loved one is not around to dazzle you, do doubts emerge?

The opposite can also be true. You may be in love with an image that is portrayed through beautifully written words. But when you are together, the reality of looks, actions, and speech makes you question your feelings. It is possible to fall in love by merely exchanging love letters. Don't let your feelings be swayed by the poetic beauty of words. And be careful not to let your own written words cause you to commit yourself to a relationship with someone you really haven't spent that much time with.

Love is stable, not up and down, depending on whether you are together or not. Unstable love is superficial. It can grow into true love, but it takes time.

3: WOULD YOU BE JEALOUS AND UPSET IF SOMEONE ELSE MADE A SERIOUS PLAY FOR YOUR LOVED ONE?

Jealousy is not a sign of true love. One of the greatest mistakes young people make is to believe that the more violent the jealousy, the stronger the love. It's normal for a fleeting thought of jealousy to occur when two people care deeply for each other. But beware of prolonged or irrational feelings of jealousy because they signify possessiveness.

People who suffer acutely from jealousy often have an underlying sense of insecurity that leads to an overwhelming need to be loved and to control the lover. As a result, a person can be extremely jealous even though he or she may not be in love at all. Love "bears all things, believes all things, hopes all things, endures all things" (1 Corinthians 13:7).

Jealousy in marriage can kill the love two people once experienced. Instead of setting the other person free to become everything God wants that person to become, jealousy constrains the other. This lack of trust, this irrational jealousy, can easily turn feelings of affection into feelings of hostility. Don't get involved with someone who is irrationally jealous before marriage. The wedding ceremony seldom makes much difference.

4: DO BOTH OF YOU HAVE A SUBSTANTIAL NUMBER OF COMPLAINTS IN COMMON ABOUT HOME, PARENTS, SCHOOL, AND OTHER THINGS IN YOUR LIVES?

Most people agree that there cannot be real love unless two persons share common interests. But being companions in misery is not the same as being in love. Marriage partners should be able to share miseries and heartaches, but such sharing is not in itself love. All too frequently couples mix up the two and enter into marriage simply because each has discovered a fellow sufferer with whom to unite against an unfriendly world.

Sometimes couples get married in order to escape an unfortunate situation. One might want to leave the abuse or conflict experienced in their parents' home. Another might want to escape a controlling parent. If this is the reason for marriage, it usually doesn't take long for couples to realize they have jumped into an equally unfortunate situation. An unhappy home life can sometimes trick them into thinking they're in love.

Nikki is a good example of this. She was constantly battling her parents. When Phil came along, she saw him as her knight in shining armor who was going to rescue her from her problems. She thought she was in love, but she wasn't. She just wanted a legitimate way to escape the control of her parents.

5: HAVE YOUR PERSONALITY, BEHAVIOR, OR ATTITUDES CHANGED DURING THIS COURTSHIP?

When you are in love, you should be happier and healthier. True love makes you want to be and do your very best. It should bring your most positive traits to the surface. Your container of love should be so full that it overflows to others.

Sometimes it is difficult to assess yourself, so ask your friends, teachers, or parents. Are you more fun to be around? Are you more responsible? Are you more thoughtful?

If your positive behavior has deteriorated, something is wrong. Are you neglecting others in an effort to focus on the one you have fallen for? This is a sign of infatuation. Give yourself time to settle into a love relationship that is so full it spills over to others. If it's really love, your friends and family will let you know. They will tell you that you are a better and happier person because of it.

6: IS YOUR RELATIONSHIP WITH YOUR PARENTS STRAINED?

A true love relationship should enhance all relationships, including your relationship with your parents. When you begin to invest your life in the life of your lover, there is a natural drawing away from Mom and Dad. You no longer spend as much time with them as you might have in the past. And you now have someone else to confide in, so your need for intimate communication with your parents is reduced. But this doesn't have to cause a strained relationship. True love should not cause hard feelings or rejection. Instead, the love you are feeling for each other should cause you to treat your parents with more kindness, thankfulness, and respect.

7: WHEN YOU AREN'T WITH YOUR LOVER, ARE YOU UNABLE TO CONCENTRATE ON THE RESPONSIBILITIES OF WORK OR SCHOOL BECAUSE OF UNHEALTHY DAYDREAMING?

If so, this is another indication of infatuation. Genuine love is centered in the other person, with your whole behavior directed toward his or her welfare and happiness. Thus, a couple in love can study and work comfortably, either together or apart, knowing they are contributing to each other's happiness. Romantic love, in contrast, is self-centered. The smitten one becomes absorbed in his or her own misery at being separated from the adored one and becomes dysfunctional. This is a sign of being in love with love. It's a sign of infatuation rather than true love.

8: DO YOU FIND YOURSELF CONSTANTLY ON GUARD TO MAKE SURE YOU ARE AT YOUR BEST WHEN YOU ARE TOGETHER? DO YOU WORRY ABOUT YOUR APPEARANCE? ARE YOU OFTEN CONCERNED THAT YOUR BEHAVIOR OR WORDS WILL BE MISUNDERSTOOD?

Love doesn't make lovers feel uneasy. If you are still trying to impress the other person, *you* are the dominant concern in the relationship, not the other person. Real love is beyond that. When you experience true unconditional love, then you know that you are loved for who you are; you feel comfortable and at ease in the other's presence. You can let down your hair and be yourself.

9: If you receive a love letter, or if your lover communicates something meant just for you, are you tempted to share his or her words with others?

Love is a private bond between two people. If one party permits intimate details of a relationship to be made public, can you imagine how that would make the other feel? This sharing of intimacies may be a bid for prestige in the group, but it shows disrespect for the lover.

10: Do you feel as close (or closer) to God now than you did before you fell in love?

Connie had never missed a week in church until she met Louie at a church picnic. It bothered her at first that Louie didn't attend church regularly. But he convinced her he got more out of staying home and watching the church service on TV or going backpacking than he did sitting in a pew. "What's wrong with skiing on the Lord's Day?" he argued. "There is nothing so inspirational as standing on the top of a mountain and looking out at God's wonderful handiwork."

Little by little Connie began to rationalize away her convictions about worshiping God in His sanctuary on His day. She convinced herself that where she worshiped God was not as important as the fact that she did worship. But when she was with Louie on his weekend outings, they rarely talked about spiritual things. Louie just wasn't interested.

Too many people try to rationalize away their spiritual convictions when their hearts want to pursue a relationship with someone who is spiritually insensitive. Many times you cannot determine whether you have similar spiritual values until you are in a dating relationship. Ask yourself if you are a spiritually stronger and better person when you are together. Is the other person seeking truth and a closer relationship with Christ? Are you able to share Christ with each other? If your relationship to Christ deteriorates in a dating relationship, then this relationship is leading you in the wrong direction and should be broken. If you continue to advance toward bonded intimacy, the chances are high that you will end up unequally yoked together.

If Connie and Louie decide to marry, there is a good chance that Connie's guilt over not being in church would lead her back in that direction, but I doubt if Louie would follow. So instead of enjoying each other's fellowship in church and growing closer together, church would become a barrier in their relationship.

11: ARE YOUR IDEALS AND MORAL STANDARDS THE SAME OR HIGHER THAN BEFORE YOU MET EACH OTHER?

When two people are infatuated with each other, instead of encouraging higher moral standards and ideals, they often settle for the lowest level that they have in common. This means that one partner usually ends up sacrificing his or her values to be accepted by the other in order to keep the relationship alive. When two people are truly in love, their desire is to become better people for each other. Instead of values, ideals, and standards going down, they usually go up as each encourages the other to become the best he or she can be.

12: DO YOU GET ANGRY AND DEFENSIVE WHEN SOMEONE DOESN'T APPROVE OF THIS RELATIONSHIP OR DOESN'T THINK YOU ARE RIGHT FOR EACH OTHER?

If so, this indicates that you want to continue this relationship, regardless of what others think. You think you know better. If you truly love another person, you will politely listen to what others are saying and willingly admit the truth of their statements. If the criticism is unjustified, you will take time to set the record straight without resorting to anger or defensiveness. True love is not easily angered (1 Corinthians 13:5).

13: DO YOU SEEK ADVICE FROM THOSE WHOM YOU ADMIRE (TEACHERS, COUNSELOR, PASTORS, OR PARENTS)?

If you truly love someone, you will want the best for that person—not just the best for yourself. Seeking the advice of others is good counsel. Others, especially parents and trained professionals, can often see areas of potential conflict that you might be oblivious to. A good marriage depends on both of you being the best for each other. Love leads you to be open to learn how this can be achieved.

If it's love for a lifetime, it will weather analysis and grow stronger because of it. And given time, others will affirm that this relationship is a positive one for both individuals. With the blessings of friends and relatives, the wedding will be a much happier event.

14: WOULD YOU FEEL GUILTY IF YOU DIDN'T GET MARRIED?

Sex is probably the biggest reason people get married before carefully assessing each other's compatibility. Petting, which leads to sexual arousal, is designed by God to culminate in intercourse. If intense petting is experienced too early in a relationship, the feelings aroused can confuse thinking. Too often guilt drives a couple to get married prematurely. Just because a sexual mistake has been made doesn't mean that one should rush into a shaky marriage. One mistake is bad enough. It's better to end a relationship at that point than to compound the mistake with a second by marrying the wrong person. God forgives and He wants you to be truly happy.

15: DO YOU KNOW HOW EACH OTHER FEELS ABOUT MONEY, CHILDREN, ROLE EXPECTATIONS, AND SEX?

True love is practical. It's often the little things that you don't think are important at this point of your relationship that will make or break a marriage. You need to seriously discuss each other's views. You should know each other long enough to observe whether what is said verbally is consistent with one's behavior. For example, Larry said he believed in saving a tenth of his salary. This led Rita to assume that he had a savings account. But weeks later she found he not only didn't have a savings account, but he also had maxed out his credit cards.

Things to talk about in the financial area: What are a person's financial priorities—tithe, family purchases, savings? What about credit cards? Who is going to handle the bills and checkbook? How do you feel about separate checking accounts?

In the child-rearing area: Do you want children? When? How many? What types of discipline should be used? What about sharing child-rearing responsibilities? Should Mom stay home? What about Dad?

In the role-expectation area: How will the household duties be divided? How do you feel about a wife working? Who should make the final decisions? Who handles the finances? Do you consider the wife's career as important as the husband's career?

In the area of sex: What are you expectations of sex in marriage? What about birth control, and what kind is preferable? Is there ever a time to withhold sex from the other? (For more questions, see the appendix.)

Romantic love often causes couples to commit themselves to marriage without really getting to know each other. Many couples involved in premarital sex have commented that their communication stopped when sex began. They ended up married without knowing how each other felt about practical day-to-day habits and happenings. Rushing the physical side of a relationship before you really get to know a person can result in a short-term commitment causing you to head down a rocky road for the first few years of marriage or get to the point of giving up and becoming another divorce statistic. How much better it is to wait until the illusion of romantic love settles into the real thing before you say yes to a long-term commitment.

SOMETHING TO THINK ABOUT . . .

- Is your relationship still under the illusion of romantic love, or do you believe you've found true love? Give some examples from your relationship to support your answer.
- Do you see some areas where you could grow as a couple?

CHAPTER 13:
MAKING YOUR DREAMS COME TRUE

The progression of your dating relationship and the ultimate choice of a marriage partner will affect your future behavior, attitudes, interests, desires, friends, job and relationship to God. Marriage is a life-changing event, one that requires a great deal of prayer, soul searching, and time. It's a pivotal point in your existence after which everything is affected.

Marriage should never just happen. It should be the most anticipated and planned for experience in your life—but it should also be the fulfillment of your dreams—and the continuing fulfillment of more amazing dreams than you ever before thought possible.

Yes, marriage has responsibilities, but it holds incredible opportunities. Marriage is a safe place to discover who you are, and it's a great place to learn to love yourself and to grow in your love for your spouse. As life happens, both the good and the bad, it causes changes in you that provide incredible opportunities for growth. What a privilege to be able to experience the pursuit of dreams and celebrate the fulfilled ones with your best friend and life companion. The question is, Who do you want to be by your side as you go on this amazing journey called life?

Fulfilled dreams don't happen by chance. Without a plan, a fairy-tale honeymoon is likely to vanish with the practical realities of marriage just about as quickly as Cinderella's coach vanished at the stroke of midnight.

How do you keep your dreams alive when so many couples today have lost the vision of what God intended marriage to be? The answer is to plan for "happily ever after" on a daily basis and to follow that plan throughout your developing relationship.

WHAT DO YOU WANT OUT OF MARRIAGE?

Now is the time to dream about what you want out of marriage. What do you want your future together to be like? Be bold. Don't shortchange yourself. Take every wonderful idea that pops into your head, sift it with reality, and write your dreams here. Dreams can come true.

1. _____

2. _____

3. _____

4. _____

5. _____

These dreams are your ideal. You may enhance them as you gain new insights of what true lifetime love is all about; just don't give them up. As you get closer to a marriage commitment, include the hopes and dreams of your loved one. Don't let the skeptics tell you that it's impossible. The fulfillment you find in marriage may actually exceed your expectations. Anything is possible. But it will never be yours if you don't believe it and don't plan accordingly.

The steps to making this dream into a reality aren't difficult. We'll walk through them in this chapter. Believe me, if you follow these guidelines during your dating, courtship, and engagement periods, you'll be better prepared to make your dreams come true.

KEEPING YOUR DREAM ALIVE THROUGH YOUR DATING EXPERIENCE

Your dream for living happily ever after starts with you. During the dating stage, the most important factor that will affect your future happiness has to do with you and the choices you make.

STEP 1: BE THE KIND OF PERSON YOU FEEL HAS "GREAT MATE" POTENTIAL.

In other words, be the best person you can possibly be. All of us can find areas in our lives that could be improved. Ask yourself what changes you would make to become a better person. Evaluate yourself in the following areas and write down your ideas for self-improvement. (If you can't think of any, ask the people who know you best to suggest some ideas.)

Spiritual:

Social (Relationships):

Emotional (Feelings/Attitudes/Personality):

Physically (Fitness/Health):

Intellectual (Education):

Financial:

STEP 2: MAKE A LIST OF THE CHARACTERISTICS, INTERESTS, SKILLS, AND ABILITIES THAT YOU WOULD LIKE YOUR MARRIAGE PARTNER TO HAVE.

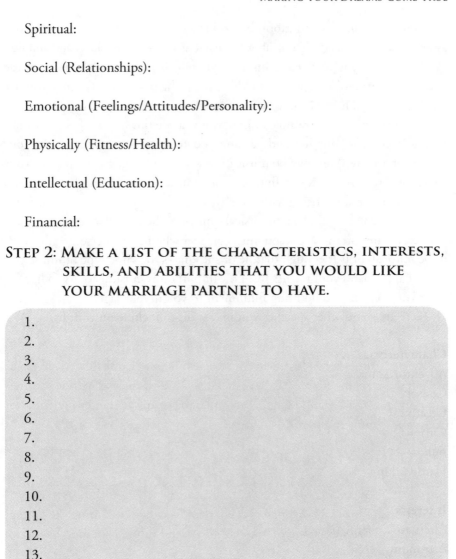

1.
2.
3.
4.
5.
6.
7.
8.
9.
10.
11.
12.
13.
14.
15.
16.
17.
18.
19.
20.

Now is the time to brainstorm beyond character traits alone. (That was your assignment in chapter 3.) Think about characteristics, interests, skills, and abilities.

Remember, you're never going to find your ideal mate in the exact shape and form you have imagined, but this list can help you clarify what you are looking for. And it can form a basis upon which you can evaluate your dates.

Let me give you an example of how you can use this list as a guide without letting it control your life and causing you to become discouraged in your search for a mate. You may be musical; let's say you sing, so you put on your "want list" that you'd like to find someone musical who could play the piano or the guitar, or at least sing with you. That's pretty specific. In your search for that person, you may find a nonmusical someone who has *all the character traits* you feel are important. Now you must consider whether the person really needs to be musical, or is it enough that he or she enjoys the same type of music you do and appreciates your talent? Just how important is musical ability in light of what you consider would bring fulfillment to you in marriage?

Here are some other specifics you may want to include on your list:

Characteristics
Adventuresome
Conservative
Creative
Curious
Fun
Hardworking

Interests
Alternative energy (going "green")
Astronomy
Backpacking
Bird watching
Camping
Flying
Mission work
Motorsports
Philosophy
Reading

Rock climbing
Running marathons
Surfing
Stamp collecting
Traveling
Water sports
Wilderness living

Skills and Abilities
Artistic
Athletic
Building
Cabinet making
Computer savvy
Financial management
Gourmet cook
Interior decorating
Mechanical
Musical
Writing

Ideally, these lists will help you get started thinking about what is really important to you. Remember, your list will change based on your dating experience. Dating helps you learn more about yourself and what you really appreciate in others. The more you date, the more your ideas will gel about the type of person you want to spend a lifetime with.

"I want to marry someone who makes me feel comfortable just being me," commented my daughter's friend. Here's what she said about her dating experience. "The first guy I dated was a perfectionist. Whatever it was—his hair, his clothing—it had to be the very best. Even though I was only in the eighth grade, I suddenly became very aware of what I wore and critical of the way my family did things because I didn't feel they were up to Tony's standards.

"Then Kurt came along. He was just the opposite. Suddenly I felt it was OK to wear old jeans and sneakers. But Kurt teased me about being a goody-goody because I didn't listen to rock music or go see movies in theaters, so I was never up on the latest hit tunes or movie releases. While dating Kurt I developed an overwhelming desire to go against the wishes of my parents, in order to better fit in with my peers.

"Then Michael came on the scene. He was not a believing Christian. I didn't know if I should say Yes when he first asked me for a date, but he was so polite. When I explained I didn't go to movies, he respected me and said, 'That's OK. I don't particularly like movies anyway. I'd much rather do something so we can talk.' I was beginning to feel more comfortable just being me—and getting a clearer idea of the type of person I wanted to marry.

"Next came a philosopher type, and suddenly I was interested in philosophy. My freshman year in college I dated a music major. And, if you can believe it, I even considered getting a music minor. Believe me, I'm not that musical.

"Now, I'm just looking for someone who will be comfortable to be around that I can just be me. And ideally, if he's the right kind of guy, I'll want to be a better person because of our love, not because I think I need to change in order to be accepted." Then she added with a look of anguish, "Do you think I'll ever find someone like that?"

My answer? "If not. Don't get married!"

STEP 3: DATE PEOPLE WHOM YOU CONSIDER TO HAVE MARRIAGE POTENTIAL.

Dating should be fun. Your goal should be to establish many friendships. Don't be so caught up in your pursuit to find the right mate that dating becomes a compulsive, joyless undertaking. Dating is a screening process. Assess your dating friends and evaluate each according to your "want list." If there are some serious flaws in one, move on and make more friends who might have more of the characteristics that you're looking for.

Don't delude yourself into thinking that someone will magically change and become your ideal. Remember, it is possible to fall in love with the wrong person—and spending all your time with this person is usually what pushes you over that cliff!

STEP 4: DON'T MAKE A LIFETIME COMMITMENT WHEN OVERCOME WITH PASSIONATE LOVE.

Wait long enough for your rational thinking to catch up with your emotions before cementing your relationship with a marriage license. In other words, make sure your passionate love mellows into true love—the 1 Corinthians 13 type of love—*before* marriage.

STEP 5: MOVE SYSTEMATICALLY THROUGH THE BONDING PROCESS.

Enjoy each gourmet course of bonding to the fullest without rushing toward the dessert of physical intimacy.

STEP 6: THROUGHOUT YOUR DATING, BE OPEN TO COUNSEL FROM FAMILY, FRIENDS, AND PROFESSIONALS.

Earnestly seek God's will for your life. Then listen to His Holy Spirit. When a red flag pops up in your mind about the relationship you are pursuing, pray *earnestly and hourly* that the Holy Spirit will make it very clear what you should do. Red flags could be the Holy Spirit's nudging. It's at those times that counsel from others may be helpful to confirm whether or not these are danger signals. Ultimately it's your decision. Do you follow what your mind is telling you, or do you go by your feelings?

STEP 7: DON'T BECOME ENGAGED UNLESS YOU ARE READY FOR MARRIAGE.

The primary function of an engagement is to plan for a wedding. If you are just starting your freshman year and don't want to get married until you graduate, hold off on the engagement. If you are currently in debt and want a few bucks in the bank before getting married, wait until you have a sound financial plan before making your intentions public.

Long engagements aren't good. Engagements should only be long enough to plan a wedding and put the final touches on your developing relationship. Talk about marriage, but don't get engaged unless you are absolutely sure this person is the right mate. And even then, as you become more intimate, you may learn things about your partner that hadn't surfaced before that may cause doubts. It's still not too late to back out. You are not married yet. Not until you say, "I do," have you made a binding lifetime commitment to each other.

STEP 8: CAREFULLY CONSIDER THE REASONS YOU ARE GETTING MARRIED.

You may say it is for love, but it could be for reasons that have very little to do with love. Some people get married for the wrong reasons.

Love, if you define it as the physical desire to be together, is not enough to hold a marriage together. Rather, marriage should occur when each person wants more than anything else to meet the other person's needs, and both are ready to commit their lives to that purpose. Marriage should happen when you're absolutely certain that the person you're dating is the person you want to be your best friend and life companion in the pursuit of all your future dreams. Here are a few of the wrong reasons to get married:

Everybody else is getting married. It's amazing the pressure dating couples experience when their friends start getting married.

Stacy and John and two other couples had been dating since their junior year in high school. These six kids had become the closest of friends. Four years later when the two other couples had gotten married and started spending more of their time with other married couples, Stacy and John began to talk of marriage. They knew they had major differences and unresolved conflicts, but marriage just seemed to be the next step in their relationship. It was what others expected of them.

Another example is Lance and Kierra. They were in their early thirties when they started dating, and neither had been married before. They became interested in each other because of their church involvement. The problem was, all their church friends were married. Although his friends didn't mean to pressure Lance, they did tease him by constantly asking, "Have you asked Kierra yet?" Lance and Kierra got married because it was the socially acceptable thing to do. Their peers practically demanded their marriage.

Industry makes a wedding look so appealing. One glance through a bride's magazine makes any young woman start to fantasize about how beautiful she will look in her expensive gown and how handsome her tuxedoed groom will be beside her. Add candles, flowers, love songs, and those exotic honeymoon hideaways that are advertised, and the thrill of a wedding becomes almost irresistible. Marriage may be good for business—but not always for a dating couple!

You don't want to disappoint the family. Jessie was a single mother. She knew her children needed a father and Gene was a nice guy. In fact, her entire family thought he was the ideal marriage partner for Jessie. But Jessie never felt Gene was quite right for her. He had a few personality quirks that bothered her, and she wasn't physically attracted to him. "Don't worry," her friends counseled, "Look how the kids love Gene. And look how much Gene loves you."

Jessie went ahead with the wedding, but she continued to harbor doubts and experience feelings of sexual attraction for other men she met. Gene has been a wonderful father to her children, but Jessie still wishes she had waited until she found everything she wanted in a man rather than making a decision based on her children's needs and her family's wishes.

Peer pressure, industry appeal, and family expectations are not the only wrong reasons for marriage. Some marry because they are getting older and are afraid they won't find anyone else. Others say, "I do," hoping to get out of a bad home situation. Others simply want independence, and they think marriage is their ticket.

But God said couples should marry so two people could become one. When you are one, you love, respect and care for the other person as you would take care of yourself. Until your love for each other is totally unselfish, it's best not to get married.

KEEPING THE DREAM ALIVE THROUGH YOUR ENGAGEMENT

Most couples look back to their engagement as a peak experience in their lives. Here is where romance blossoms. Love may begin in the dating and early courtship stages, but now the intensity builds. Someone loves you, and it's no longer a secret. Those nightmarish times of wondering if you would ever "catch" the man or woman of your dreams is past. You are now looking forward to your wedding and to living together for the rest of your lives. You have found security.

But the engagement period is not all candlelight and roses. You have some serious work to do if you are to keep your dream alive during this time.

STEP 1: KEEP NURTURING YOUR RELATIONSHIP BY LOVING ACTIONS.

There is nothing like the overwhelming feeling of love—the joy, the fulfillment, the excitement it brings. Affection is a wonderful thing. The desire to be near, to touch, and to hold is awesome. But the strong feelings of attachment you have for each other at this moment will remain and grow only if you handle them with care.

Feelings are capricious. They come and go. They fluctuate minute by minute, hour by hour. They can change in a moment with a harsh word or even a what's-the-matter-with-you kind of sigh.

Some justify their negative behavior by saying they can't control their feelings.

Or they let their negative feelings crowd out the positive ones. Slowly love and affection can turn to frustration and resentment and eventually to hate and rejection. That's why so many people fall out of love. And why so many marriages end up in divorce.

Of course, you may not be able to control the initial onset of an emotion, such as fear or anger, but you can control whether you will allow that emotion to continue to affect you or hurt another person.

How do you control your feelings? The answer is, with your actions. I once read a book titled *Love Is Something You Do*. I've since forgotten the contents, but I've never forgotten the truth of the title. Love is something you do. It's the words of respect you speak, even when you feel resentful. It's the kind things you do for each other, even though you feel like playing dirty. It's going the extra mile, even when you don't like it or feel you're being taken advantage of. It's choosing to see the positive in the negative. It's anticipating new opportunities for growth that hurt, pain, or suffering might bring.

Don't allow your feelings to control your actions. Feelings are ephemeral. If your actions are always actions of love, this environment will allow you to create the life you want. You might have to get creative, but all the resources you need are around you.

Learn how to love. Learn what makes your beloved happy. Learn how to put your love into words. Learn how to reach out and be a helpmate to each other. During your engagement, learn everything you can about what makes happy, successful, fulfilling marriages, and begin to put these things into practice. You'll notice that something wonderful will begin to happen. You'll discover something about who you are and what the awesome power of God is able to create in your life. Your feelings of love for each other will grow, and you'll find that mountaintop experiences of love are out there just waiting to be discovered.

How do I know this works? Because of what Jesus said in John 13:17. "If ye know these things, happy are ye if ye do them" (KJV). Always remember that God's formula is knowledge first, actions second, and feelings third. In other words, you first have to know what to do. Next, you have to trust God and do what you know you should. And finally, happiness and fulfillment will be the result. Basically, principles of love *when practiced* will result in positive feelings.

STEP 2: DON'T GLOSS OVER POTENTIAL PROBLEMS BECAUSE YOU ARE TOO BUSY PLANNING THE WEDDING, COMPLETING YOUR EDUCATION, OR EARNING ENOUGH MONEY TO GET MARRIED.

This period in your relationship can be hazardous. If you're not careful, an engagement can sweep you into a marriage before you're really ready. When troublesome things surface, it's tempting to gloss over the problems, knowing that the wedding date is fast approaching.

Most people think that engagement automatically leads to marriage. A healthier mind-set would be that the engagement commitment to marry is conditional. In other words, if you and your fiancée agree to marry only if your love for each other continues to grow and you find no reason during your engagement not to get married. If this is your understanding with each other, you will give yourself the time you need to work on troublesome issues, so you can go into marriage without reservation.

But before you consider breaking your engagement, understand that every couple has premarital jitters. Sometime during engagement, it is typical to have a few doubts about whether you are making the right choice. These feelings are natural. But if you begin to see a number of things in the behavior of the other person that worry you, the wedding date should be postponed until these conflicts can be resolved. Time and physical separation have a way of helping make it clear which way you should ultimately go.

Kent and Marie had a very stormy engagement. Five days before the wedding, Kent was impressed that the wedding shouldn't take place, but after talking to his fiancée, he decided to go ahead with it. Why? Because he had made an engagement commitment to Marie and didn't feel he should break it. He loved Marie enough not to hurt her.

The result was an even stormier marriage. At one point both even considered suicide as a way out. The only thing that saved them was making a renewed spiritual commitment. Now both Kent and Marie are so committed to the Lord and spreading the gospel that this common interest holds them together.

Once you have announced your engagement to friends and family, it is extremely difficult to break up and not feel guilty or embarrassed. When engagement parties have been celebrated or shower and wedding gifts start to arrive or the wedding invitations have gone out, some people feel that their doom has been sealed. It's too embarrassing to call things off.

But it's not too late. It's better to be embarrassed and wait until you are sure than to enter marriage with unresolved doubts and end up divorced five years later.

Expense is a big reason weddings aren't called off. Bridal gowns must be ordered four to six months before the wedding. Bridesmaids may already have gone to the expense of buying or making their dresses. Engagement pictures and wedding invitations cost money. You may have gotten nonrefundable airline tickets for your honeymoon, or relatives and friends may have already purchased tickets to come to the wedding.

How can you avoid these pitfalls of the engagement that hurl you more quickly toward a wedding than you are ready for?

Here are some ideas:

Don't announce your engagement until you have had premarital counseling. The counseling should include taking personality tests to determine compatibility and problem areas. Then if certain troublesome issues surface during these sessions, you will be able to take the time you need to resolve these differences.

Don't be afraid to voice your doubts and discuss the possibility of postponing the wedding until things smooth out. It's a lot better to go slow and make sure your relationship is stable than to rush toward a preset date and end up spending your first few months or years of marriage going through the adjustments you could have worked through before.

STEP 3: DISCOVER EACH OTHER'S HIDDEN SECRETS.

Now is the time to find out everything about your potential mate. There is reason to be concerned if there are secrets or parts of his or her life that are taboo topics. If the road ahead is not yet clear of yesterday's garbage, consider this a warning signal. If your fiancé/fiancée feels that the risk of sharing his or her past is too great, then insist he or she sees a counselor. While you don't have to know the specifics, you should talk to the counselor to determine if the problem could be a potential hazard in marriage.

During the engagement period you'll want to evaluate the minor things you find irritating about each other and ask yourselves whether you can live with these things. Marrying a person for his or her good traits is not good enough. It's the faults that get under your skin and begin to make you doubt whether you've got the right mate. And don't be surprised if some of these things don't surface until you are well into the engagement period. Some of us become masters at hiding our faults when we want to make a good impression. But marriage isn't an act, and usually within a few weeks, we become who we really are. It's certainly better to make this discovery *before* the wedding date.

It's important to discover how the person you are marrying reacts in a time of crisis. What's truly in a person's heart usually comes out during a crisis. By going through some hard times together during your courtship, you'll know if your relationship has what it takes to weather the storms of life.

How are conflicts solved between the two of you? This is another important area to evaluate. If you're not satisfied with the process of resolving conflict that has developed in your relationship, take time to get some professional help so you can learn a better way. If one partner characteristically gives in to the other, don't expect this to last much past your honeymoon! If one gets angry and goes silent, it's tough to solve problems. Is this a pattern you want to live with for the rest of your life?

How responsible is this person for his or her own happiness and fulfillment? If your fiancé is so wrapped up in you that you become responsible for making him or her happy, that's a pretty heavy burden to take upon yourself. Of those couples who do, few make it beyond the first year or two.

I've only talked about a few of the significant things to discover during the engagement period. As you grow, you'll discover even more. Don't be afraid to deal with those issues. If you take the time now, when those wedding bells ring, you can say without a shadow of a doubt that you have chosen God's ideal for you.

Remember this counsel: "Through wisdom a house is built, / And by understanding it is established; / By knowledge the rooms are filled / With all precious and pleasant riches" (Proverbs 24:3, 4). Be wise as you move through these significant stages of serious dating, courtship, and engagement, for your goal is to have a home where the rooms are filled with all "precious and pleasant riches." That's my dream for you. I hope you will make it your own.

SOMETHING TO THINK ABOUT . . .

- Are you and the one you love on the road to "happily ever after"? Explain your answer.
- Have you set specific goals for your relationship to get where you want to go? If not, why not set aside time in the next few weeks to make some plans for marital bliss? You'll be glad you did.

CHAPTER 14:
LETTERS AND A FINAL MESSAGE

Most parents whose children are seriously dating or engaged would like to share their wisdom and observations about love and marriage with their kids to guide them through this time. But many don't know how to go about it so their kids will listen. Your parents probably feel the same way. Sometimes it helps to write down what you really want to say. As you read the next four letters, imagine that your parents are writing to you. The fifth letter is one you might want to write to your own parents. And finally, I close the book with an important message all parents want to give their adult children. It's a must read!

LETTER 1: FROM MOM TO HER SON WHO IS IN LOVE

My Dear Son,

Just yesterday, it seems you were whispering in my ear, "Mommy, when I grow up, will you marry me?"

I remember replying, "Of course, but what about Daddy?"

Today you are grown up and in love. What happened to those little-boy years? I've been wondering if I have told you everything you need to know to move into your future with a firm step. Are you ready for love's responsibilities?

Walk carefully through the next few months and years. Love is a beautiful thing, but there will be challenges that you should be aware of. For example, never again will your behavior be so governed by feelings. Don't let them rule your life. They will undoubtedly whisper things to you that may seem right at the moment, but in the long run they will prove foolish.

God created you with the marvelous capacity to perform sexually, and the one you love probably has only a dim idea about the power she has over you in this area. The way she dresses, her flirting eyes, her caressing touch, her soft voice—any one of these things can make you forget about all the sex education classes you've ever taken. So during your courtship, you must be in control.

180

You must be her guide, not her slave. You must set limits and not depend on her alone. You must make responsible decisions, even though you feel like throwing caution to the wind.

It's not easy to say No when your body, the world, and your friends are saying, "Just do it." Our sinful environment has made sleeping together almost as common as a goodnight kiss—and living together an accepted alternative to marriage. You will be tempted to compromise your standards. But by putting this marvelous courtship experience into a lifetime perspective, you'll find that restraint and wisdom now will ensure an abundant and fruitful harvest of love in the future.

As much as possible, avoid situations where your values could be compromised, such as spending hours alone in her home, in your apartment, or in your car. You are the one who must monitor your relationship. She may not always agree with your prudence, but she will respect you for it.

God has made clear His recommendations of what is appropriate before marriage and what is to be preserved for after the marriage feast. Remember the counsel of Solomon that there is a proper time for everything. He also said, "Can a man hold fire against his chest and not be burned?" (Proverbs 6:27, TLB). In matters that are irreversible, it is always better to be on the conservative side. Learn to deny present pleasures for future benefits.

The most precious gift in the world is your bride-to-be. Don't mar her beauty. Treat her with honor and deep devotion for the gem she is. Don't be tempted to do anything that might cast a shadow on her reputation—or yours. Never ask her to compromise her standards. Speak to her with words that are pure and fit for royalty. Don't let the media pollute your vocabulary of love. How a woman is treated will determine what she becomes. Treat your beloved with esteem, and she will become your esteemed.

You determine how fast or how slow your relationship will grow. Don't rush her into a lifetime commitment prematurely. Grow together, enjoy each other, laugh, sing, be crazy together, and encourage her to become everything God wants her to be. Marriage is for a lifetime; it's worth waiting for.

Have I trained you how to lead and not to manipulate? Have I told you how destructive control is to the precious gift of love? Have I told you how important unconditional acceptance is in a love relationship? Can you accept her just the way she is? Will you love her even if she may not keep herself as trim and attractive as she is now? What if she isn't a good cook and housekeeper? Will you love her just the same? What if she can't have children? Can you live with her through the ups and downs of her monthly cycle? It's so easy to withhold love from a person if she doesn't behave the way you think she should. It's easy for a man to lecture or push his opinions. Can you, in love, hold your tongue—and at the same time express your true feelings? Learning this art is essential for a good marriage.

It's your responsibility to guide each date. Do you surprise her with little gifts, a flower, or a poem? It's a nice habit to get into before marriage. Do you plan interesting activities so you can get to see each other in different situations? Do you go places with others? It's important to interact with others during your courtship so you can see how you react in different social situations. And do you pray together? A man is to be the spiritual leader of the family. What better place to start than when you are dating. Have you thought of starting each date with a prayer, or maybe ending it that way? That may be even more meaningful than a goodnight kiss—well, it might be!

Encourage her to listen to the counsel of her parents. Get to know them. Seek their advice and be open to their concerns. They have her best interests in mind. When you've decided that you definitely want to get married, ask them for their blessing. Someday you'll look back and say, "That was the best advice my mom ever gave me!"

Son, you are very special to me and always will be, but once you're married your loyalty must be to your wife. God's advice is clear, "Leave . . . and cleave." So although I'm sending you this letter now, my role as chief advisor in your life is just about over. You must now look to each other—and to God to determine what is best for both of you.

My prayer is that you will follow God's timetable for your life and that you will find true love and joy as you and your beloved begin a new life together.

With special love, Mom

LETTER 2: FROM DAD TO A SON WHO IS IN LOVE

Dear Son,

The news that you're in love with the girl you want to marry brought back great memories of when I first fell in love with your mom! I wish I knew then what I know now about how to treat a woman. I'm writing down a few of the lessons I've learned so you can be smarter about love than I was! Here goes:

Lesson 1: *Little things are important.* We men tend to focus on cosmic things: politics, sports, science, technology, religion, philosophy. Chances are your girl may be a lot more interested in small things like whether or not you remember her birthday or put down the toilet lid. Watch her body language for how she's feeling. It's probably a lot more accurate than her words. Notice the little things that evoke her look of disappointment, the shrug of her shoulders, or how she rolls her eyes. "I'm sorry. I had no idea this was important to you," works a lot better before marriage than after. You better start taking notes. Because after marriage, little things like forgetting that welcome kiss or not patting her rump may mean you'll find yourself sleeping on your own side of the bed until you figure out what you did wrong and apologize. And the longer you wait to admit your error, the more expensive the "forgive me" gift has got to be. The guy who wrote the book, *Sex Begins in the Kitchen,* knew what he was talking about! Remember, to win a woman's heart, there is no job that a man shouldn't be willing to do. That includes little things like washing dishes, making beds, or removing messy diapers, vomit, and the garbage!

Lesson 2: *Listen.* There are few things woman enjoy more than shopping and talking. They can do the shopping by themselves, but the talking requires someone to listen. That's YOU, Son! I've found that a woman stores up an unbelievable number of words during the hours that you're apart. So, when you first get home, sit down, look her in the eyes, hold her hand, and LISTEN. You think that you can listen when you're looking through the bills or reading your e-mails, but she knows that's impossible. So don't try to fake it. If you want to make both of you happy, plan a thirty minute daily talk time away from the TV, radio, iPod, cell phone, or kids. Some couples have swing time (sitting on the front porch swing). Others, a foot-rubbing session, a moonlight walk, or pillow talk.

Lesson 3: *Learn her love language.* Marriage has taught me to not presume that the woman you love thinks the same way you do, nor does she feel loved in the same way you do. Once I heard about the concept of different love languages, I had a much better understanding of how to love your mom. Some people feel loved by physical intimacy, while others enjoy quality time, gifts, acts of kindness, and meaningful communication. Unless you know how your mate feels loved, the chances are you will try to show love in the same way as you feel loved. That works—if you both have the same love languages. But that rarely happens. So learn her love language—and daily say "I love you" in the way she understands.

These lessons should help you become the man—and lover—that your wife needs you to be. I want you to know, I trust that your words and actions leading up to your wedding day will be honorable and trustworthy. For right now, that's probably the most important way to keep her love and respect for you growing. God has a wonderful plan for your future. Hold on to Him—and each other—and enjoy the ride.

I love you, Son. And I'm mighty proud to be your dad.

LETTER 3: FROM MOM TO A DAUGHTER WHO IS IN LOVE AND WANTS TO GET MARRIED IMMEDIATELY

My Precious Daughter,

I'm excited with the news that you have fallen in love with a very special man. I wish I could be with you to celebrate and share what's on my heart. But since I can't, I have decided to write.

First, I want you to know just how much I love you. Being your mom has meant everything to me. I remember praying for you; the ecstasy of a positive pregnancy test, and the excitement of your first intrauterine kick. Finally your birth and the joy of watching you grow more beautiful each day. What an honor! What a delight! And now you're all grown up and have fallen in love. And you're thinking about marriage. How does a mother let go of her prized jewel without at least a few words of wisdom that I've gleaned over the years?

You are experiencing passionate love for the very first time. I'm happy for you, but concerned you might rush this wonderful experience. Love, like good soup, needs to simmer. Putting it on too hot a burner will ruin it. I want you to relish each day for what God has in it for you. Don't rush God's timetable.

Marriage is for a lifetime. Too many couples get married when they are so passionately in love that they aren't thinking clearly. If this happens, when the passion settles—as it will with time—you'll have to live with those decisions. Will you have the spiritual, intellectual, emotional, and social bonding necessary to hold your relationship together? Will you have truly married your best friend?

If one races through love to a lifelong commitment, some things are missed: relationships with others who will be your social network and support in the future; courses of study that could enrich your life a hundredfold; intellectual stimulation from long discussions on life issues; cultural experiences—art, music, drama—that make you a well-rounded person. Young adulthood is a time of rapid expansion and change. Don't shortchange your life. I want you to have everything that is coming to you. I want you to have every good thing.

You will sacrifice so many things if you insist on a passionate race toward marriage. Don't let passion control your life, driving you into marriage before you have a chance to become the person you are in the process of becoming. True love is not controlling or manipulative. True love is disciplined. It's a choice. And it takes time to develop. That's why one's first passionate experience with love doesn't always last. That's why true love isn't always experienced in marriage—and why marriages so often fail.

My precious daughter, you can have everything. In God's time, it will all come together like the pieces of a puzzle—if you don't rush biology. Right now everything in your being desires a physical relationship. You must accept these feelings, but not necessarily give in to them. And you must be wise beyond your years not to put yourself in a position where these feelings of attraction move more quickly than you want.

"But Mom," I hear you say, "just because others get in trouble, doesn't mean we will. We really love each other!"

I know you do, sweetheart, and only you can determine the status of your relationship. Just remember, if your relationship causes you to want to isolate yourselves, if you are only happy when you are together, if you aren't drawn closer to your family, friends, and God, then your relationship is probably in the passionate stage.

To be fair to each other, you need to give yourselves time to let your love permeate into the other areas of your lives. Let it be a part of your total growth, intellectually, professionally, spiritually, and socially. If not, it's easy to look back someday and blame each other for opportunities missed. If you want the strength of true love that will bind two people in a lifetime commitment, you must not move too quickly.

I know you want to make wise choices. I know you have in the past, so don't think that I don't trust you now. It's just that you've never experienced these strong feelings of love before, and they can give mixed and unhealthy signals without your realizing it. You can't know this unless you've gone through it, and that's why I so much want to help you. Your first experience with love is so important. I just want to give you some input. I'm like a caution light that says, Slow down through this significant time, until you are very sure you have God's green light for marriage.

Time has benefits. You'll discover whether or not your friendship will continue to grow. Do your personalities mesh? Are your interests similar? Do you respect each other?

Respect may be more important than passion for a lifelong commitment to marriage. Do you respect his initiative? His personal devotional life? His career ambitions? His knowledge? His intellect? His vocabulary? His mannerisms? His friends? His leadership ability? The Internet sites he frequents? The choices he makes about the use of his time? His interest in current affairs? His interest in developing various talents and skills?

And does he respect you in these areas as well? Does he inspire you to develop your God-given talents? To aim high? To pursue your calling and mission?

How do others feel about your relationship? Do they think you are right for each other? Do their opinions matter?

Most important, I want you to know that I love you as a part of me. You don't have to do anything to be loved and accepted, and the choices you make will never change that love.

Just because I voice my concerns and say what I feel, doesn't mean that this is correlated in any way with my love for you. You do not have to do what I advise in order for my love to continue.

I set you free. You hold your future. God has blessed you with many gifts. How you choose to develop your intellect and your abilities, and how you apply your skills to life and a profession is entirely your choice. If you just take time to let God's Spirit lead, you'll be everything God intended you to be. And you will experience love to the fullest. That's what I want for you. When you have definitely decided this is the person you will marry, I will rejoice with you for the love you have found. I just want your relationship to develop in such a way that it will be easy to love your choice of a partner for the rest of your life.

You are my special child. You always have been. And I want you to have a special future with a very special man. Whatever you decide, I want you to know I'll always love you.

Your Mom

LETTER 4: FROM DAD TO A DAUGHTER WHO IS IN LOVE

Dear Daughter,

Regardless of how grown up you are, I want you to know that you'll always be my little girl. Like the words of the song . . .

You're the end of the rainbow; my pot of gold,
You're Daddy's little girl to have and to hold.
A precious gem is what you are,
You're Mommy's bright and shining star. . . .
You're sugar; you're spice; you're everything nice.
And you're Daddy's little girl.

Whatever happens in the future, wherever you live, or whatever you do, always remember, God loves you even more than I do. Because you are the daughter of the King of the universe, you are royalty. Christ died for you, redeemed you and calls you His bride! Your value is priceless. Never forget that—and live accordingly.

I'm writing to you because you have found someone special to love and adore. That man is the luckiest guy in the world. But before I "give you away," here are some words of wisdom from your good old dad about what a husband needs from his wife.

1. *Loyalty.* My role as advisor is quickly coming to an end—marriage demands that you "leave" your folks and cling to each other. Regardless of how close you've been to Mom and me, your primary loyalty must be to your husband. Loyalty means there are some things that you don't share with anyone else. I'm not talking about putting up with abuse. It should never be tolerated. What I am talking about is that when you're married, you stick up for each other against the world. You are ONE. Your husband needs to know you love him so much that you would give up everything and would be willing to go to the ends of the earth with him. Loyalty demands that he'll do the same for you.

2. *Encouragement.* There will be days when things go wrong—career disappointments, failures, rejection, unrealistic pressures to perform, accidents, health problems, and bad choices with negative consequences. A man needs a woman who sees possibilities—not problems, who has a mind-set of hope, who

views failure as a stepping-stone to success, and who believes with all her heart in the truth of Romans 8:28, "All things work together for good. . . ." Encouragement is salve to a bruised and broken spirit. When a man is down, he needs an upbeat woman. Two discouraged people are like the equation $0 + 0 = 0$. Nothing is gained when two are down in the dumps together. But if one will always choose to be positive, then $0 + 1 = 1$. Discouragement sees only a slammed door; encouragement sees a dozen new doors of opportunity opening. That's what marriage is all about. Together you will create opportunities for growth, for self-fulfillment, for reaching your God-given potential. And when the going gets tough, encouragement keeps your marital ship on course.

3. *Companionship.* You can either choose to be a married single, or a married couple. Couples do things together. They like each other and are best friends. They love being together. At first, it's easy to find the time. But as children come along and home and career responsibilities increase, you will need to choose to do things with your husband—camping trips, football games, tennis, hiking—or you'll end up getting left behind. A man needs a recreational companion—that's one of the reasons he gets married. Learn to enjoy what he enjoys—and ideally, he'll do the same for you. Be fun to be with. The more you do together, the more you'll learn about each other, and the closer you will become. Marriage doesn't guarantee companionship. It's a choice you make on a daily basis.

4. *Respect.* Don't marry to have your needs met. Two needy people don't make good marriage partners. But at the same time, it's important to know that, in love, you will choose to meet those needs. I can't think of a more important need within marriage than the need for respect. When you respect yourself, others will respect you, and you'll treat others with respect. Love is patient and kind—never thoughtless and abusive. Love grows and thrives only if planted firmly in respect. The secret for finding fulfillment in marriage is to treat your mate with respect, both in private and in public. In your words and actions, let him know he's your knight in shining armor. In return, he'll love, nurture, protect, and care for you. That's the way God designed marriage to work. Check out Ephesians 5:21–33.

5. *Forgiveness.* Even though you love each other very much and you think you've found the perfect mate, remember he's human. Over the days and years to come, he'll probably do things that will irritate and upset you—and you'll do the same. Don't let these little irritations—these little molehills—become

mountains. Settle them quickly, laugh, hug each other, forgive, and move on. And sometimes it's not just little things. Regardless, forgiveness is the only road to reconciliation. When it's your fault, be quick to say "I'm sorry, please forgive me." When he's in the wrong, be quick to say, "You're forgiven." In case you're tempted to hold a grudge because you don't think he deserves your forgiveness, it's not worth it. It will eat you up and put poison darts into your relationship. Remember, forgiveness is always a gift—and God loves a cheerful giver!

Well, there you have it. I hope these few tips will help you find your heart's desire in the man that you love so much.

Your loving Dad

LETTER 5: FROM YOU TO YOUR PARENTS WHEN YOU BEGIN DATING SERIOUSLY

Dear Mom and Dad,

I love you and I always will, even though my relationship to you is changing. Don't be hurt if I forget to call or if my letters no longer tell everything. And if I don't happen to make it home for Christmas, please understand. I'm not trying to hurt you. I'm just trying to get in touch with myself and what's happening inside. I am becoming me—a person separate from my childhood family; a person who is seeking to establish a home and family of my own.

I feel a magnet pulling my heart and allegiance away from you and from the home you provided for me. I thank you for your love, the sleepless nights, and your endless prayers on my behalf that guided me to this point.

I can never repay you. I can, however, continue to become the person you and God want me to become. However, since I have never gone this way before, my efforts toward becoming my own separate self may be clumsy. Try to understand and don't judge me too harshly.

Right now I need you to listen more than I need you to tell me what to do. I know you want what is best for my life. And you give good advice. I will always respect you for that and will listen to you. But please don't preach. And don't expect me to automatically accept what you say. I need time to consider your options, to seek others' counsel, and to finally come to my own conclusions. You have done a good job in training me to think for myself. Trust your work. Trust me.

I know you would like to have a say in who I date or choose for my lifetime marriage partner. I can understand that, especially after all the time, money, love, and prayers you have invested in me. But this must be my choice. I will have to live with this person. I promise I will not make a hasty decision, nor will I make a commitment before we seek premarital counseling to determine our compatibility; I don't want to make a mistake either.

I know that when I fall in love, good sense, at least for a while, is likely to depart. I expect you to say whatever is necessary if you see me in danger. I may not like it, but don't get mad at me if I get mad at you, OK? Somebody needs to keep their cool. I know my rationality will return and I'll be sorry for expressing my angry feelings. And when that happens, please forgive me. I'm still learning.

You have taught me God's commandments and the importance of living a pure and moral life. I want to honor God with my life, and I don't want to do anything that will cheapen the relationship I have with the person I choose to marry.

Thank you for your prayers. I need them. And thank you for your unconditional love. I'll love you always, even when I give my heart and life to another. Thank you for letting me grow away from you, that I might grow stronger and more mature.

With love always,
Your kid!

A Final Message from Your Parents

Gloria and Bill Gaither's song "Some Things We Must Tell the Children" beautifully expresses all the messages parents try to get through to their children, such as watching your diet, minding your manners, hanging up your clothes, and making your bed. But the years go by so quickly. And although your parents probably found time to teach you how to tie your shoes, ride a bicycle, and brush your teeth, I wonder if they took the time to communicate to you the most important message of all—the message that you are loved.

As you read the words or listen to the Gaither song, some of you will say, "Those words aren't from my parents." Parents make mistakes—sometimes tragic mistakes. Some are abusive or neglectful, and some of you are carrying physical and emotional scars that only the Lord can heal. But deep down in the heart of every parent, even though it may be buried under a load of depression, bitterness, or hostility is the desire to give you this message.

You are no longer a child. You are in love, or will be soon. In just a short time, you will be establishing your own family apart from your mom and dad. Your parents know these years are significantly important for you because they have gone through them themselves. But they can't live your life for you. They must set you free, and trust God *and you* as together you make the most important decision of a lifetime—whom you will marry. This choice will either bring you fulfillment or frustration. This choice will influence who you will become. This choice will fashion your future and determine your destiny.

Here are your parents' parting words . . .

How can we tell you the things we must tell you
About choosing your lover for life?
To keep yourself pure and seek God's advice
So you won't have a lifetime of strife.

We trust you to live as we've taught you to live,
And we now set you free to decide
Who you choose to date, and whether to wait
For the right one to stand by your side.

But whatever you do, we'll still pray for you,
And we'll pray for the person you choose.
And when you marry your mate, we'll all celebrate.
Just some things we must tell the children.

I hope you're listening.

LEADER'S GUIDE FOR *SERIOUS ABOUT LOVE*

Instructions: *Serious About Love* can be used in a thirteen-week seminar/ discussion group or for an ongoing youth support group. The following are suggested discussion questions to get your group interacting about what they've read. These questions can also be used after viewing each session of the *Serious About Love* DVD seminar. (Ordering instructions are giving at the end of this Leader's Guide.)

SESSION 1: WHAT DO YOU WANT OUT OF MARRIAGE?

Introduction: Marriage is a pivotal point. In one way or another, everything beyond it will be affected by the one you choose as your mate. Choosing a marriage partner who will stand the test of time is the most important decision you will ever have to make. Yet many people are more serious about checking out the car they want to buy than the person they want to marry. Can you imagine buying a car on feelings alone?

1. How do you feel about this statement: "Marriage is a lifelong commitment to a one-flesh relationship, regardless of personality, handicaps, temperament, money, looks, or health. This commitment shouldn't be hard to keep. It shouldn't be work!"
2. What is the difference between putting effort into marriage and seeing it as hard work?
3. What do you want out of marriage? Here are some possible ideas: romance, intimacy, companionship, a sense of fulfillment, someone to love you, children, security.
4. What should you do before marriage to prevent a relationship from becoming one of convenience?
   a. What about after marriage?
   b. What might be the first signs of a devitalized marriage?

c. When the first signs appear, what should you do about it?

5. What should you do before marriage to prevent a devitalized relationship?
   a. What about after marriage?
   b. What might be the first signs of a devitalized marriage?
   c. When the first signs appear, what should you do about it?

6. What should you do before marriage to prevent a dominant/submissive relationship?
   a. What about after marriage?
   b. What might be the first signs of a dominant/submissive marriage?
   c. When the first signs appear, what should you do about it?

7. What should you do before marriage to prevent a conflict-filled relationship?
   a. What about after marriage?
   b. What might be the first signs of a conflict-filled marriage?
   c. When the first signs appear, what should you do about it?

SESSION 2: DATE THE RIGHT MATE OR BEWARE OF YOUR FATE

Introduction: It's easy to fall in love. Most people fall in love many times before they are really serious about love—often with individuals who would make very poor marriage partners. Obviously you won't marry everyone you fall in love with, but the chances are quite high that you will promise to love, honor, and obey someone you will date in the next few years.

1. Is it possible to be madly in love with the wrong person?
2. Is being in love reason enough to marry?
3. Have you ever heard someone say after the first date or two, "I could never fall in love with him," or "She's not my type" and then end up marrying that person? Why do you think that happens?
4. Is it possible to fall in love with almost anyone? If yes, how does it happen?
5. What's the difference between friendship or casual dating and serious dating?
6. What would you say to a person who continues dating someone just because he or she is lonely?
7. How can you protect yourself from feeling a relationship is God's will

when there are definite indicators that it isn't?

8. What does it mean to be double bonded?

9. How can you tell when you are dating if one person is overly dependent on the other? What might be some signs?

10. Why is it dangerous to marry your counselor or counselee?

11. How can you know whether the person you are dating has unresolved conflicts from the past?

Divide into three groups to discuss "Dangerous Dating."

    Group 1: Internet Dating

    Group 2: Avoiding Date Rape

    Group 3: Red Flags to a Potential Abusive Relationship

Discuss the following questions:

- What experiences have you had or have you heard about that would confirm the dangers written above?
- What other cautions would you add?
- How do you feel you can best avoid the dangers so your dating experiences can be safe, meaningful, and God-centered?

SESSION 3: WHAT ARE YOUR CHANCES OF BEATING THE ODDS?

Introduction: Research shows that you will have the best chance of staying married—and being happily married—if you marry someone who is similar to you in age, race, cultural values, education, spirituality, and interests. Headstrong love makes a couple think they can beat the odds and find happiness and lifelong fulfillment in marriage regardless of what the research says. But before committing your life to another, prayerfully consider your age, racial, cultural, spiritual, and educational compatibility.

1. Do you agree or disagree that opposites attract? Explain your answer.

2. When opposite attraction results in marriage, what is the result?

3. How do you feel about age differences when it comes to marital happiness?

4. How do you feel about racially mixed marriages?

5. How might cultural differences affect the happiness of a marriage?

6. How important is it that a couple have the same spiritual values?

    a. How can you determine whether you do or not?

    b. How important is it that you belong to the same denomination?

7. How might educational differences affect a marriage?

8. What is the ideal length for a courtship? For an engagement?

9. What are the problems that might arise if parents disapprove of the marriage? How can these be dealt with?

10. What if all other advisers think this is a good marriage yet parents still disapprove? What should you do?

SESSION 4: QUALITIES OF A GREAT DATE

Introduction: List the traits you want to find in a mate, and then divide your list into two categories: (1) Those traits that are absolutely essential, and (2) those that would be nice—but you could live without them. Discuss why one trait is important for one person but not for another.

1. Why are the following characteristics important to have in a potential mate?

    Trait 1: A happy disposition

    Trait 2: Thoughtfulness

    Trait 3: Not easily angered

    Trait 4: Willing to solve problems

    Trait 5: Purity

    Trait 6: Truthful

    Trait 7: Good health habits

    Trait 8: Accepts responsibility

    Trait 9: Good sense of self-worth

    Trait 10: Likes children

    Trait 11: A personal relationship with God

    Trait 12: Accepts you just the way you are

    Trait 13: Willing to grow

    Trait 14: Affectionate

2. In your group, what traits were mentioned on individual lists that are not among the fourteen traits listed above?

3. What does the group feel are the three most important traits for a potential mate to have?

4. How important is attractiveness or good looks to a fulfilled marriage?

5. What if looks change during marriage because of illness or an accident? How do you think this might affect your feelings?
6. When might good looks become a negative factor in marriage?

SESSION 5: HOW TO BE A GREAT MATE

Introduction: Finding the right person will not necessarily insure marital happiness; being the right mate, however, may. So before going in search of your Mr. Right or Ms. Perfect, why don't you take a good look at yourself and ask, "Would I make a great mate?"

1. How essential is marriage to your happiness in life? How essential is marriage to fulfillment of your life expectations?
2. If you suffer from low self-value, what can you do to increase your self-value and acceptance?
3. Write down the traits about yourself that you feel pleased about. Write a statement telling yourself how great you are in a certain area. Read it to a friend. How did it make you feel when you shared something positive about yourself? Have the other person affirm that positive statement.
4. What is the relationship between accepting yourself and accepting others?
5. Are there things that have happened to you in the past that have caused you to develop traits that may be considered by others as offensive or potentially troublesome? What should you do now to deal with those issues so they will not get in the way of your having a happy marriage?
6. What is gift love? How might this type of love become detrimental to marital happiness? What can you do to overcome perfectionism?
7. How can you determine if you are making wise and mature decisions?
8. How can the development of your spiritual life contribute to marital happiness?

SESSION 6: TANGLING WITH THE TEMPERAMENTS

Introduction: Read the list of traits in each of the four temperament styles and circle those that describe you. In which area did you circle the most traits? Analyze previous relationships you have had. Did you choose to date people with similar traits as yours, or different?

Sanguine: outgoing, talkative, friendly, optimistic, enthusiastic, cheerful, spontaneous, creative, sincere, curious, sense of humor, childlike, controlled by circumstances, becomes angry easily, doesn't hold grudges, life of the party, enjoys being up front, volunteers for jobs, spontaneously touches others, loves to be around others, inspires others, people oriented.

Phlegmatic: easy going, relaxed, calm, patient, sympathetic, kind, competent, steady, agreeable, avoids conflicts, not easily upset, quiet, keeps emotions to self, good under pressure, has many friends, compassionate, observant, inoffensive, easy to get along with, puts off duties and solutions, dislikes change, takes time to talk and listen.

Melancholy: deep thinker, analytical, serious, conscientious, idealistic, artistic, enjoys beautiful things, persistent, orderly, perfectionist, self-sacrificing, economical, enjoys details, easily depressed, pessimistic, avoids attracting attention, suspicious of others, content to stay in background, makes friends cautiously, devoted to others, good listener, easily moved to tears.

Choleric: natural leader, delegates work, motivates others, well organized, confident, dynamic, active, strong-willed, independent, not easily discouraged, goal or product oriented, practical, little need for friends, bossy, is usually right, difficult to see own faults, impatient, unemotional, enjoys controversy, sees the whole picture, excels in emergencies, tends toward being a workaholic.

1: What are the strengths and weaknesses of each temperament?

2: Discuss what an individual can do to overcome weaknesses in a particular temperament style. What I've written below will help you get started.

Sanguine:
1. Think of others before yourself.
   - Make others feel special by remembering names and birthdays.
   - Listen to others.
2. Plan and organize your life.
   - Prepare for future events.
   - Pay more attention to details.
3. Carry your fair share of responsibility.

- Stick to one project until finished.
- Delegate when appropriate.

Phlegmatic:

1. Pull your fair share.
   - Be observant about what needs to be done.
   - Don't put off doing things.
2. Show motivation and enthusiasm.
   - Try something new.
   - Laugh, smile, and show positive emotion.
3. Solve problems when they arise.
   - Learn to talk through problems rather than retreat.
   - Share negative feelings rather than bottle them up.

Melancholy:

1. Enjoy every day.
   - Be more spontaneous and do things that are pleasurable.
   - Take time to cultivate and enjoy friendships.
2. Cultivate the positive.
   - Resist the temptation to gossip.
   - Count your blessings and express thanks.
3. Accept yourself (and others) as human.
   - Don't be discouraged with imperfection.
   - Accept others unconditionally.

Choleric:

1. Accept the fact that no one is perfect.
   - Learn to apologize and say, "I'm sorry."
   - Don't pressure others into your high-performance standard.
2. Learn to relax.
   - Take time for fun activities and making friends.
   - Plan leisurely activities.
3. Cultivate patience.
   - Don't expect immediate solutions.
   - Encourage others' ideas and choices rather than forcing yours.

Session 7: Enjoying the Single Life

Introduction: Read the lyrics (or if you know the tune, sing), "I Wish I Were Single Again." Do you know anyone who has ever said, "I wish I were single again"? Why do you think they said it?

1. How do you feel about being single? If you knew now that you would never get married, how would that make you feel?
2. What advantages are there in being single?
3. How can you get the most out of your single years?
4. What can you do during your single years to best prepare for marriage?

Session 8: How to Break Up and Remain Friends

Introduction: No one enters a serious dating relationship anticipating a breakup. You expect fun, companionship, and romance. When romance is on the rise, there is an exhilarating feeling that nothing could ever go wrong. But it can. The element of romance seldom lasts forever. In that grey area between romantic illusion and true love, breaking up is a real possibility.

1. If you knew a relationship were going to break up after a few months, what would you do to ensure a soft landing after the breakup?
2. Is it possible to prepare for a breakup? What "parachutes" would you hang onto so the breakup would not destroy you or the other person?
3. Is it possible to break up gracefully? How?
4. When someone breaks up with you, what are the five don'ts you should remember?
   - Don't
   - Don't
   - Don't
   - Don't
   - Don't
5. Is it possible to break up and still remain friends? If so, do you know anyone who has done this? How did they do it?

SESSION 9: SYMBOL OF A LIFETIME, ONE-FLESH COMMITMENT

Introduction: Tara and Jon are in love—a true, committed love. And lately they've been feeling some pressure. The hugs are arousing strong responses, and the kisses are becoming more intense. They wonder if waiting until marriage for sex is really necessary, or just an old-fashioned concept. After all, they're totally committed to each other. They're mature, intelligent adults. They know all about safe sex and birth control. And they're planning on being married someday.

1. How would you answer the questions young adults like Tara and Jon are asking?
   • What's wrong with sexual intercourse before marriage?
   • Is oral sex outside of marriage permissible?
   • How far can we go before we've crossed the line?
   • How can something be wrong when it makes us feel so good?
2. Why did God create sex?

SESSION 10: GROWING TOWARD BONDED INTIMACY

Introduction: Many sexual relationships are entered into because of the mistaken idea that intimacy can be achieved only by having sex. But true intimacy is not physical—it's psychological. It can be psychological and physical, but never just physical. Because sex and intimacy are erroneously equated, too many lonely people jump into bed with strangers and end up dreadfully disillusioned. It is the foundation stages of a relationship that make true intimacy possible.

1. What is bonded intimacy?
2. What are the four relational stages of bonded intimacy?
3. How is friendship dating different from serious dating?
4. What steps within the various stages would you consider most important for the achievement of psychological intimacy?
5. What is the major danger of rebound romances?
6. Is a person's first love experience different from others? If so, how?

SESSION 11: COURTSHIP COMMUNICATION

Introduction: It doesn't take long for a lack of communication to destroy a marriage. That's why it's important to learn the principles of good communication during your courtship. Now is the time to listen for the feelings behind the words, tune into body language, and learn how to say what's on your mind. With a little thought and some training, you can smooth out the rough edges of what you say so you can get your message across without causing hard feelings and becoming frustrated.

1. What is the difference between *talking* and *communication*?
2. What is good communication?
3. How do you know when you are really communicating with another individual?
4. Why is it so important to share your feelings?
5. Which of the principles of courtship communication do you find most difficult to achieve?
6. Think of a problem a couple would argue about. First, role-play the typical argument. Second, replay the situation using I-messages (Principle 7) and problem-solving steps (Principle 8).

SESSION 12: DISCOVERING THE DIFFERENCES BETWEEN ROMANTIC ILLUSIONS AND TRUE LOVE

Introduction: How do you feel about the following statement?

"Romantic love or infatuation is short term and has only the passion. It's a totally absorbing type of love, blinding two people in a whirlwind of bliss and makes them oblivious to reason and reality. Romantic love is blind!"

1. What kind of problems can you expect when you proceed with a wedding based on romantic love rather than true love?
2. How can you determine the difference between romantic love and true love?
3. What can you do if you discover your relationship is based on romantic love—and you want a lasting relationship?
4. Does romantic love always become true love if given enough time?
5. If you had a son or daughter who was romantically in love and

planning a wedding, what would you do? Can parents do anything to slow down a relationship? Should they?

6. What responsibility do friends have to warn a couple if they feel they're rushing into marriage without the foundation of true love?

SESSION 13: MAKING YOUR DREAMS COME TRUE

Introduction: Marriage should be a dream come true, but fulfilled dreams don't just happen by change. Without a plan, a fairy-tale honeymoon is likely to vanish with the practical realities of marriage just about as quickly as Cinderella's coach vanished at the stroke of midnight.

1. Describe a married couple you know who has a relationship that you'd like to have with your spouse some day. What do you like about their marriage?
2. Fairy tales always end with, "And they lived happily ever after." Is that possible with marriage?
3. Is it possible to have too high expectations of marriage? What is the benefit of having a dream?
4. How do you feel about this statement: "Ideals are like stars; you may never reach them, but you can set your course by them"?
5. When is it too late to call off the wedding?
6. Divide into six groups. Have each group chose one of the following letters (messages) found in chapter 14 to read and discuss the following questions: How did the letter make you feel? What was left out? If you were writing a similar message, what would you say?

   Group 1: Letter 1: From Mom to a Son Who Is in Love
   Group 2: Letter 2: From Dad to a Son Who Is in Love
   Group 3: Letter 3: From Mom to a Daughter Who Is in Love and
        Wants to Get Married Immediately
   Group 4: Letter 4: From Dad to a Daughter Who Is in Love
   Group 5: Letter 5: From an Adult Child to Parents
   Group 6: A Final Message From Your Parents

Note: This Leader's Guide can be used either as a discussion based on reading this book, or it can be used as a discussion guide following the viewing of the *Serious About Love* DVD seminar featuring Dr. Kay Kuzma and Dick Duerksen. This entertaining and informative DVD series contains 13 thirty-minute programs. The *Serious About Love* DVD seminar is available from AdventSource by calling 1-800-328-0525 or 402-486-2995; on the web at www.adventsource.org, or by writing AdventSource, 5040 Prescott Avenue, Lincoln, NE 68506. AdventSource also offers a seminar discount when ordering 25 or more of the *Serious About Love* books.

APPENDIX:
TOPICS TO DISCUSS BEFORE MARRIAGE

Here is a list of questions that you and the one you love will want to discuss before marriage. The topics are arranged alphabetically and are not in any order of importance. You can use this list throughout your courtship to stimulate conversation, or as a reference to see if there are some topics you have not yet considered. It's important to enter marriage with as much information about your mate as you can possibly obtain so your decision to marry will be guided by common sense and not passion. Discussing these questions now could save you from some unpleasant surprises in the future.

ATTITUDES

ATTITUDES ABOUT MARRIAGE

What is the purpose of marriage?

Why do you want to get married?

Why are you interested in marrying now?

How do you think marriage will affect your life?

What adjustments or changes will you have to make in the way you live?

What goals do you have for your marriage?

What does a lifetime commitment to marriage mean to you?

What is the difference between legal separation and divorce?

How do you feel about divorce and remarriage? What does "biblical grounds" for divorce mean to you? Are there any other grounds for divorce that you feel are acceptable? Should couples stay together just because of the children? What effect does separation or divorce have on the couple, children, or the extended family?

What would you do if your mate had an affair? How might this affect your marriage?

What should couples do to promote or maintain a feeling of oneness?

How important is romance in your life? What should couples do after marriage to keep romance alive? Is romance necessary to a good marriage? Explain your answer.

Should you get married if you are in debt? If so, should both husband and wife take equal responsibility for paying off the debt even though one person did not benefit from it?

How do you feel about a wife retaining her maiden name? How about having both husband and wife combining both of their names as their married name?

When one or both have lived a promiscuous life before marriage, what consequences might their previous lifestyle have on their marriage?

ATTITUDES ABOUT YOUR RELATIONSHIP

What are the three most important reasons you want to marry each other?

What expectations or dreams do you have for each other? What about further education? Degrees to be earned? Career advancement? Athletic, musical, or artistic achievements? Honors or certificates of achievement? Other?

Thinking ahead ten years, what kind of person do you think your mate will have become? How do you picture your mate twenty-five years from now? What about yourself?

What are three characteristics you feel are most important in order to be a good spouse? Parent? Son- or daughter-in-law? Do you see these traits in your potential mate?

If you could change something about each other, what would it be? Do you feel comfortable in discussing these things, or do you fear hurting each other's feelings?

Do you feel you will be able to change your mate? How?

When you are together, what makes you most happy? What does the other person do that makes you feel loved?

When you are together, under what conditions do you feel most proud, comfortable, secure, insecure, afraid, embarrassed, or frustrated?

In your relationship, what has hurt your feelings or made you unhappy? Why do you feel you reacted like this? Do you see this situation happening again? How do you think you will react if it happens again?

How do your friends and family view your plans for marriage? How do you wish their views were different?

Is there anything that could happen that would make it difficult for you to continue to love each other? For example, what about becoming fat, bald, impotent, physically handicapped or disfigured, addicted to drugs, alcohol, or pornography? What would you do if any of these things happened?

How do the two of you react when emotionally irritated? Are you satisfied with this behavior in each other? How do you wish it would change? What are the three things that annoy you most about each other? What are some things the other does that offends you?

How important do you feel it is to keep each other informed regarding schedules and whereabouts?

How much should you share with a mate about work, other interests, controversial opinions, and negative feelings (hurt, jealousy, rejection, guilt, doubt)?

How important is it that you are able to discuss intellectual and emotional issues with each other, such as race relations, politics, religion, and current affairs? Are you satisfied with the discussions you have had so far in these areas? Are you satisfied with the level of information the other person brings to the conversation? Do you feel your potential mate is over- or under-opinionated? Does this bother you? What was the most recent situation in which you wished your potential mate was more open to another opinion rather than defending his own?

In a love relationship, what kind of sacrifices should you be willing to make for each other? Should you give up your career if it conflicts with your mate's value system? Would you be willing to give up your job if a move to another location would mean a career advancement for your spouse? What about your educational goals? What about the way you enjoy spending your leisure hours? (If you're a weekend TV football addict and your mate hates it, what should you do? If you love to shop and your mate doesn't, how will you handle it?)

How do you feel when you are separated from each other? How do you think you might react after marriage to long-term separation because of a job or the illness of a parent? How would it affect you if your mate's job required long-distance traveling? Does absence make the heart grow fonder? Why or why not?

What gifts do you enjoy receiving?

What are the ways that make you feel most loved? Physical touch, intimate communication, receiving gifts, someone doing kind things for you, quality time together?

How important are the following to your happiness in marriage?
- Humor
- Love surprises: gifts, special dates, etc.

- Appropriate public display of affection
- Politeness and manners
- Willingness to compromise
- Seeing counseling for unresolved problems
- Being able to depend on the other
- Overlooking faults rather than criticizing
- Unconditional acceptance of each other

Other Attitudes That Might Affect a Marriage

How do you feel about authorities who tell you what to do (e.g., the police, the government, the military, parents or grandparents, school or church leaders)?

How do you feel about various professions, such as lawyers, psychologists, doctors, etc.?

What type of a career do you want to have? Do you see yourself being self-employed, in a business partnership, joining a family business, part of a reliable big firm, or part of a small hometown company? Do you see yourself as a chief executive officer, a department head, or merely a capable employee?

How important do you feel further education and/or training is for you to reach your career goals?

Do you have strong opinions about social issues, equal rights, woman's liberation, the welfare system, and labor unions?

How do you feel about abortion, euthanasia, prayers in public school, giving out contraceptives in high school clinics, individuals with AIDS serving in health professions, world hunger, global warming, and other hot topics of social concern?

How do you feel about public affection and intimacies before marriage?

How do you feel about signing prenuptial agreements?

CHILDREN

Do you want to have children? How soon after marriage? How many? Sex preferences? Which first? How many years should be between children?

Is there any reason to question whether you will be able to have children?

How do you feel about adoption? Foster care?

How should children's names be selected? What are your favorite names?

What strong convictions do you have about how children should be raised? What type of discipline should be used and who should administer it? What should you do if you disagree with each other on how to discipline a child?

If you could look ahead fifteen years, what kind of children would you like to have? What would your family look like? What dreams do you have for your children? What special lessons would you want to provide for them? How important is reading, travel, music, art, or sports?

What educational aspirations do you have for your children?

What are your feelings about public versus private education? Would you consider home schooling?

What responsibility should children assume to pay for their own education?

What are your feelings about homework? Should parents become involved in school activities?

How do you feel about a woman working during pregnancy? For the first year or two after the baby is born? When the children are preschoolers? School-age? Teenagers? After they have left home?

How do you feel about a father being the primary caretaker of the children?

What are your feelings about day care, babysitters, or live-in help? How often should the children be left with others?

How involved do you think you should be with influencing your children's friendships? What ideas do you have about developing positive character traits in your children?

DECISION-MAKING

What is the best way you have found to solve disagreements?

What does the concept of the husband being the head of the household mean to you? What does the idea that a wife is to be submissive mean to you?

How should decisions be made? Who should make the final decisions in the family? Should everything be decided together? What is the role of compromise?

Who should decide the following? (Answer either husband, wife, or both. Compare your answers with those of your potential mate.)
- The date and time of the wedding
- The type of ceremony and reception
- The location of the honeymoon and how long it should be
- If you should have children—and when
- The number of children
- The selection of the children's names
- The frequency of intercourse
- Type of contraception used
- Who should initiate lovemaking
- Whether counseling is needed for unresolved problems
- Who to go to for counseling
- What church to belong to
- How involved the family should be in church activities
- What should be done for family worship times at home
- If the husband should go to school; get a job; change jobs; quit a job
- If the wife should go to school; get a job; change jobs; quit a job
- Where to live
- What type of housing is needed

- When to buy a home, a car, or other major purchase
- What home to buy
- How to decorate the home
- Who keeps the house in order
- Who takes responsibility of home repairs
- Who maintains the yard and determines landscaping
- Whose name the home and mortgage should be in
- What car to purchase
- Making arrangements for car repairs
- Maintaining the car
- How you stand on political issues
- Arranging social events and keeping the social calendar
- Frequency of going out together
- How weekends and vacations are to be spent
- How much money should be allocated to different items in the budget
- What type of insurance to get
- Financial decisions about investments, savings, etc.

FINANCES

How do you feel about joint checking accounts versus separate accounts? Should all income and resources be pooled, or should his income pay for certain items and her income pay for others?

Who should pay the bills? Who should handle the checking account?

How should decisions be made for small versus large expenditures?

How much insurance do you feel a family needs (life, medical, travel, etc.)? What about term-insurance?

How do you feel about giving tithes and offerings, or donations to special missions and/or for community needs?

How do you feel about loaning to or borrowing from friends and relatives?

How do you feel about paying cash versus using credit or getting a loan?

What's your opinion about the proper use of credit cards?

How do you feel about going into debt for the following: the purchase of a home, a car, furniture, education, clothing, or household conveniences, leisure activities such as a boat, a motor home, a vacation?

How important is it to you to have a savings account? What types of investments would you like to have? Have you thought about setting up a retirement fund or a trust for the children's education?

How you ever lived within a budget? How successful was your experience? How do you feel about budgeting? How would you feel about going to a financial planner or a financial seminar to help establish a practical budget and a financial plan for your family?

How do you feel about get-rich-quick schemes?

How do you feel about multilevel marketing plans?

How do you feel about legalized gambling: the state lottery, slot machines, Las Vegas, etc.?

How do you feel about doing things yourself versus hiring services such as house cleaning, gardening, car repair, carpet cleaning, window washing, swimming pool care, etc.?

What is your attitude about a wife working outside the home? How do you feel about a wife making more than her husband? Should a family move for a wife's career?

Are there some jobs that you feel aren't appropriate for women (such as politics or the military)?

What would you do if you got into financial difficulties?

How do you feel about bankruptcy?

How important is it to have a will? What things would you put in your will?

PARENTS

What things have you observed in your parents' marriage that you would like to have in your own? What would you definitely not want?

What memories do you have of your childhood?

What family traditions, traits, or experiences do you feel might affect your marriage? How?

What kind of a relationship did you have with your mom, dad, stepparents, grandparents, or other family members who were significantly involved in your childhood, and teenage years?

Were you adopted? How did this affect you? How do you feel about your birth parents? Would you like to contact them? Did you ever live in foster care or with someone other than your parents?

How were you disciplined and how did you feel about it?

Did you live in an alcoholic or dysfunctional home? Have you ever gone to counseling because of this? How do you feel this has affected you today? How will it affect your marriage?

Did you ever feel your parents (or some other adult) abused you verbally, physically, or sexually? How do you feel about this experience? How do you feel it might affect the way you treat your own children?

How close are you to your parents and family now?

Do you have any hostile or negative feelings about your family? How do you think these feelings might affect your marriage relationship?

Did you feel you were loved unconditionally or conditionally (loved only when you were good or did what your parents wanted you to do)? How do you feel this has affected your feelings about yourself and the decisions you have made? How might it affect your marriage?

How involved do you feel you should be in your parents' lives after your marriage? Would living with them ever be a possibility? What about living near them? How close is too close? How often should you visit or call them? Should you spend weekends or vacations together? What are your parents' expectations in this area?

When your parents can no longer take care of themselves, what arrangements do you feel would be best for them and your family?

What things about each other's parents do you dislike? What do you like?

If your parents were to give three reasons why they wanted your potential mate to join the family, what do you think they would say?

If a parent and your mate disagree, whose side should you take? Do you see any potential in-law problems that could cause conflict in the future?

How do you feel about seeking parental or in-law advice? When? How would you feel if parents or in-laws were continually giving advice without your asking for it?

Do your parents ever say anything to you that makes you feel guilty or inadequate? What do they say? How often does this happen? How do you handle these feelings?

Personal Habits

Eating

How do you feel about eating breakfast? A midnight snack? Eating between meals? How important are regular meal times for you?

When do you eat your largest meal?

What do your typical breakfast, lunch, and supper consist of?

What foods do you dislike? What are your favorite foods? Do you have food allergies? How do you feel about junk foods, sugar, preservatives, processed foods, white flour, sodas, caffeinated tea or coffee, aspartame, MSG, supplements?

Do you have any special dietary needs, such as sugar-free, low-fat, low-cholesterol, or low-salt meals?

Do you enjoy cooking and/or baking? How do you feel about cooking from scratch versus using convenience foods?

How often do you go out for dinner or lunch? Where are your favorite places? What do you usually order?

HEALTH HABITS

How often and how long do you exercise?

What kind of exercise do you enjoy most?

How do you feel about smoking and social drinking?

Do you have any addictive habits: smoking, chewing tobacco, alcohol, drugs, caffeine, coffee, or chocolate?

How do you feel about taking over-the-counter drugs or prescription drugs versus using natural remedies?

How willing are you to make lifestyle changes that could improve your health and longevity?

HEALTH HISTORY

Are there any medical problems in your family's background that could affect your marriage?

Are there any genetic peculiarities or abnormalities in your family?

Does there seem to be a history of mental illness, bipolar disorder, depression, bed-wetting, attention deficit disorder, or suicides in your family?

What diseases or health problems have members of your family suffered or died from?

Have you ever had any of the following: cancer, heart disease, diabetes, allergies, asthma, skin rashes, alcoholism, enuresis (bed-wetting), encopresis (bowel soiling), obesity, miscarriage, colitis, ulcers, osteoporosis, eating disorders?

At what age do elderly family members tend to die, and from what causes?

Have you ever had contact with someone that makes you worry about the possibility of having contracted a sexually transmitted disease, such as genital warts, herpes, gonorrhea, or AIDS?

Have you ever required emergency medical care or been hospitalized? Why?

Have you ever suffered from depression or entertained thoughts of suicide?

Have you ever seen a counselor or therapist? Why?

SLEEPING

How much sleep do you need every day?

What time do you like to go to bed and wake up?

Do you ever have trouble going to sleep? What do you do about it?

So you snore, grind teeth, sleep talk, or sleep walk?

What size and type of bed do you prefer now? What about after marriage?

Do you like an open window when you sleep?

Are you a light or heavy sleeper?

RECREATION

PAST

What types of friends did you have during your growing years?

What types of activities did you participate in together?

Did you ever get into trouble? Disobey the law? Get arrested?

What is the most painful experience you ever had with a friend?

Did you have difficulty making or keeping friends?

What did your friends especially like or dislike about you? Did you ever get teased? Why?

When did you start dating? How often? What kind of people were you attracted to? Describe a typical date.

How did you handle breakups? Which one of you broke up? Are you still friends with any of your past boyfriends or girlfriends?

How physically involved did you routinely become with a boy- or girl-friend?

Do you still have dreams about or strong feelings for anyone you used to date?

What was your most serious relationship?

Were you ever engaged or married? Why was the relationship broken? Who broke it? How long did it take your feelings to heal?

Have you ever been pregnant and had a baby or aborted one? Have you ever fathered a child?

Present

How do you feel about each other's current friends? Do some individuals bug you? Why?

Do you resent the amount of time each other spends with his or her friends in relationship to the amount of time spent together?

Future

After marriage, how much time should be devoted to former friends?

How do you feel about having personal friends rather than friends you both can enjoy? How important is it to have mutual friends after your marriage? What can you do to find mutual friends? How will you decide if these friends are good for your relationship?

How would you feel if your mate chose to do something with a personal friend rather than with you? What would you do about it?

Are there certain friends your mate-to-be has now that you wouldn't want him or her to have after the wedding? Why?

Religious Issues

What is your family's religious heritage? Do you want to pass this same heritage down to your children?

How have your parents' religious values and training affected your personal religious attitudes?

Have you had a conversion experience? What difference did it make in your life? Have you always had a close relationship with God? Describe your journey with the Lord during the last five years. How would you evaluate your personal relationship with God? Are you satisfied with it? What changes would you like to make in the future?

How do you feel about various religious issues, such as faith, prayer, baptism, Sabbath observance, righteousness, evangelism, speaking in tongues, hell, etc.?

How comfortable do you feel praying, reading the Bible, discussing Bible doctrine, or worshiping together with your potential mate?

How do you feel about church membership and attendance? How often should you attend? What services?

How involved would you like to be in a local church? What leadership positions would you enjoy holding?

How do you picture God? Jesus? The Holy Spirit? Do you ever have trouble picturing God as a loving and forgiving God?

Do you feel God calling you to a special mission?

SEXUAL VALUES AND EXPECTATIONS

What impression do you have of the sexual fulfillment, or lack of it, your parents found in marriage? What have you noticed in their home or their behavior that makes you feel this way? How do you feel this has affected your own sexual desires and expectations?

How important do you feel sexual fulfillment is to marital fulfillment? How important is it to you to experience intercourse on your wedding night? How often do you think a couple should have sexual relations? Do you feel sexual fulfillment is dependent on orgasm? Is simultaneous orgasm important? Do you have any thoughts about various positions in intercourse? What have you found to be sexually arousing to you? Are you comfortable with touch?

How do you feel as you think forward to the sexual experience in marriage: fearful, excited, anxious, curious, eager?

Have you had any previous sexual experiences that were unpleasant? What about sexual abuse? How do you feel this will affect your marriage?

What forms of birth control do you prefer? Why?

How do you feel about seeing each other nude? Is there anything about your body that is embarrassing to you?

How do you feel about stimulating your mate's body by hand or tongue? What are your feelings about oral stimulation?

Do you think you will feel comfortable communicating to your mate your sexual desires and telling your mate what is stimulating to you and what is not? Is it difficult for you to talk about personal sexual matters? Do you fear your mate won't understand? Or do you feel if you make suggestions that you will hurt your mate's feelings? What would make you feel more comfortable talking about these things?

What are your feelings about intercourse during menstrual periods?

What type of an environment do you think you would prefer for lovemaking: music, candles, perfume, incense, soft music? How important is privacy? What time of the day do you think you would prefer?

What will you do if you discover some type of sexual dysfunction in your relationship (e.g., for a man, premature ejaculation or difficulty maintaining an erection; for a woman, painful intercourse or inability to experience a climax)? What should you do if you find that your mate doesn't enjoy sexual intercourse and tries to avoid it? When should you seek sexual therapy? Who would you feel free talking with about sexual problems?

SPECIAL OCCASIONS

What kind of family occasions should be celebrated? What about family reunions? How often should they be held?

How do you feel about celebrating Christmas, Easter, and other holidays? How should these be celebrated?

Are there any special cultural or family rituals that you want to pass on to your family?

How important are birthdays? Should you exchange gifts? What gifts do you like or dislike? Flowers, cologne, practical household things the whole family can use, personal things like an article of clothing?

Thinking Ahead

How do you think you would react to the following situations if you should happen to face them sometime in the future?

- Mate sulks, pouts, or remains silent for a long period of time
- Mate is not willing to share what is obviously bothering him or her
- Mate spending time with a former girl- or boyfriend
- Mate is not as affectionate as you would like
- Mate contracts a major illness or has a disabling accident
- Mate doesn't listen
- Mate suffers from feelings of low self-worth
- Mate loses a job and can't or refuses to get another
- Mate hits you in anger
- Mate verbally abuses you, saying things that make you feel inferior or worthless
- Mate won't take responsibility around the home
- Mate criticizes you in public
- Mate does something illegal or dishonest
- Mate is convicted of a crime and goes to prison
- Mate lies to you
- Mate quits a prosperous job and goes into own business
- Mate's job changes from a day job to a night job
- Mate makes foolish purchases and causes the family to go into debt without your knowledge
- Mate tries to control you with anger, criticism, or withdrawal of love
- Children come before you planned

- You have two or three more children than expected
- A friend starts making passes at your mate
- Mate is no longer interested in spiritual things or chooses to join a denomination that you feel doesn't believe biblical truth
- Mate begins drinking too much or becomes an alcoholic
- Mate becomes addicted to harmful habits: smoking, drugs, pornography, gambling, sex
- Mate begins showing signs of an eating disorder
- Mate begins eating unclean meat (see Leviticus 11) or unhealthful foods
- Mate begins gaining weight
- Mate brings home friends that have a bad influence on your children

VALUES

What character traits do you enjoy most in others? What things about people do you dislike the most?

List the five most important things in your life.

If you inherited a million dollars, what would you do with it?

If you could spend twenty-four hours with any person, living or dead, who would you choose? Why?

If you had a choice between taking an extra job and earning some extra money or spending that time with your family, what would you choose?

How important is it that you get to the top of the career ladder in your field?

If you could live anywhere in the world, where would it be?

How do you feel about living in the city, suburb, or country? How much land would you like to have someday?

Do you enjoy taking care of a yard, having a vegetable garden, or having a backyard swimming pool?

What is your favorite vacation place? What do you like to do on vacation?

What pets would you like to have? How do you feel about indoor versus outdoor pets? What pets would you definitely not want?

WEDDING CEREMONY

Why is a wedding ceremony important? What should it mean to a couple? What do you want it to mean to you?

Where would you like your wedding to be held?

How much money do you think you would like to spend on your wedding? In what ways do you think you could "cut corners" and save money and still have a memorable wedding?

How many guests would you like to invite? How many attendants?

What do you want to say in your vows?

How do you want your guests to remember you on your wedding day?

Describe a perfect wedding day.

Describe a perfect honeymoon.

IF YOU APPRECIATED THIS BOOK, YOU'LL WANT TO READ MORE FROM KAY KUZMA.

The First 7 Years
Kay Kuzma

What you do during your child's first seven years will dramatically shape the rest of his or her life.

In this book, Kay gives parents the information they must have for meeting children's needs in the critical areas of love, individuality, emotions, discipline, cognitive learning, moral character, and personal value. Parenting is an incredible journey that you can never take again. Let *The First 7 Years* be your roadmap and travel guide to help get you where you want to go. With it, you can enjoy the parenting journey as your children grow into vibrant, loving, gentle people with strong values and principles who will love God, respect you, and bless humanity.
ISBN 13: 978-0-8163-2087-5
ISBN 10: 0-8163-2087-X

Passionate Prayer
Brenda Walsh with Kay Kuzma

Brenda Walsh is one who has learned by experience the power of passionate prayer. This book is filled with miracle stories of God's intervention in her life and in the lives of those for whom she has prayed. These exciting first-person stories will amaze and inspire you.
ISBN 13: 978-0-8163-2214-5
ISBN 10: 0-8163-2214-7

3 Ways to Order:
1. Local—Adventist Book Center®
2. Call—1-800-765-6955
3. Shop—AdventistBookCenter.com

© 2009 Pacific Press® Publishing Association
Please contact your ABC for pricing in Canada